HOPE for Parents Who Have LOST CHILDREN

*A Medium's Communication
with Children in Heaven*

It is my hope that
this book brings you
comfort and peace.

Geoffrey Jowett

Love is eternal.

Illustrator: Stephen Gardner
www.stephen-gardner.com
Photographer: Stephen Gorme
www.stephengorme.com

ISBN: 1-4392-4906-7
ISBN-13: 9781439249062

Visit www.booksurge.com to order additional copies.

Table of Contents

Special Notice to the Reader

This book was designed with outcomes to help you heal through the transformation of Your Child into Spirit. Please read it with your heart, more than your head. The Children of Spirit and my own Spirit Guides and Angels provided me with much of the information that is contained in this book. Much of the information was presented in readings, through meditations and general life experiences. The names and specific details of each reading cited in this book were changed to respect the integrity of each person receiving a reading (and Their Child in Spirit!). The content and theme of specific readings was varied but the wisdom was carefully preserved to help you on your journey of healing, light and Divine Love.

Acknowledgements

My Spirit Guides led me to some important wisdom found in books and movies from authors which are listed in the back of this book. It is through the wisdom of Edgar Cayce, Eckart Tolle and many others that I was able to comprehend and understand the messages provided to me from the World of Spirit. It is also with the beauty of the movies from The Walt Disney Corporation that these messages can help touch your heart. A very special thanks to James Van Praagh, a leader, teacher and pioneer in making us aware of the World of Spirit and providing me with countless opportunities and support to be a medium.

Foreward

Much of the information in this collection of true-life stories has been accumulated through my past readings with grieving parents, through personal meditations, and through general life experiences.

The names, and some very personal details, have often been slightly altered so as to respect the privacy and the particular sensitivities of parents who hire me to read for them and to protect the identity of their departed child who – by leaving the planet – has become their eternal Spirit Child.

While you may find some content and identities to be varied by your author, the theme and specific wisdom are carefully preserved to help guide you on your own journey to begin and complete your healing, to protect your sanity, to give you hope and to furnish you with a sense of Divine Love's eternal light, light that will clear your outlook and provide comfort on your pathway.

This book's paramount desire is to help heal YOU, or someone you know, because you are dealing with the physical loss of Your Child – be they infant, youngster or even older in age – and in Spirit (to be out of sight is NOT to be out of life!).

Many parents ask me 'Why did my child have to die?' Not one of my answers is meant to be glib. It's my heartfelt wish that I could sit with you, personally, and tell you exactly why your son or daughter had to have such an early "EXIT" on this stage of life, but I want to present to you what I found to be some of the most prevalent reasons that our children leave us too swiftly when we thought they would be around many more years – remember, please, a dear Mother named Rose Kennedy had to lose Joseph, Jr., John, and Robert – although all her "boys" were men, they were still her "babies", and it is difficult for any parent to let go of her/his child regardless of how many years they have been on this planet.

Below are SIX of the most outstanding reasons that children leave us:

1. They have learned their lesson and they feel there is no more reason to stick around.

2. YOU have learned the lesson (they were sent here to teach YOU) and they feel there is no longer a reason to hang around in the physical.

3. They were in a lot of pain and torment and they could not take pain any more (that "PAIN" is not to put a guilt trip onto you, you did everything to comfort them).

4. Sometimes a boy or a girl is not meant to last on this planet any longer than we can keep them – a lot of times, "it's just NOT 'our call' to make" as to how long.

5. Their "contract" isn't necessarily made with YOU – their contract was made with a UNIVERSE that is larger than you and them. Your Child, was never your 'property', you were simply entrusted with their care, feeding and nurturing until they returned to the SOURCE that granted them to you in the first place.

6. Sometimes a child "leaves" in order to raise the awareness of the ENTIRE plane (think of Anne Frank, Joan of Arc, the boy of "Pay It Forward")!

All these explanations may seem cool to you – they may seem detached and downright heartless – I don't want you to be left comfortless – it's just that: If you are looking for a "tailor-made" reason you might want to listen very carefully to a psychic medium, or you might want to listen very carefully to your OWN internal voice that will provide you with the truth.

Please read this book with your heart more than your head, and please read the words that follow, with an open mind. Accept only what feels right to you. Much of the information in this book is provided through my personal Spirit Guides, my Angels, and by the Children in Spirit who have departed Earth and returned to the realms of Heaven and to the Source of All Life – incarnate or otherwise. May you find hope-giving wisdom in the following text.

Blessings to you and those you love, and who love you in this world and from the World of Spirit!

Geof Jowett
Long Beach, California
June, 2009

Introduction

"No one can be uncheerful who has a balloon."

– Winnie the Pooh, paraphrased

*"If ever there is a tomorrow when we're not together...
there is something you must always remember. You are
braver than you believe, stronger than you seem, and
smarter than you think. But the most important thing
is, even if we're apart...I'll always be with you."*

— *Winnie the Pooh*

Love is the purest and highest frequency of energy. The love that you have for Your Child is powerful, eternal and sacred.

No matter what Your Child does, where Your Child is, how Your Child lives or dies, your love cannot be compromised, devalued or eliminated.

To love Your Child is to live.

There are no boundaries, no limitations or barriers that can prevent your love for Your Child (except within your own mind).

This book is written to help you understand that you and Your Child will never be separated.

I will present concepts not of my own but of many great masters, Children in Spirit, and children in the angelic realm who have taught the truths of Love and *the continuity of life*.

Some of my earliest memories are of archangels Michael, Gabriel, and Raphael, and several Spirit Guides, who repeatedly visited me while

I was a child. Many mornings, as I stood in my crib, they would assure me that they were going to be with me and would help me heal people in ways that I did not yet understand. They opened my mind to the potential of communication, wisdom, and Divine Love in the beautiful and serene World of Spirit. I was told 'miracles are natural' and that each day I would create, participate in and enjoy miracles. A thousand miracles happen everyday but only those who look for them find them along the way.

My Spirit Guides spoke the truth because my life has been blessed with many incredible and awakening experiences that include numerous, unique and fulfilling opportunities while I was escorted into the unseen World of Spirit.

As a medium and intuitive, I provide the opportunity for communicating with your departed loved ones and your Spirit Guides.

Children have always had a special affinity for me and I can relate very well to their vibrations. It can be a very healing and enlightening experience to have a spiritual reading so that you might get a better perspective about your life, your soul's journey, and you might learn how to maintain your connection to those who have crossed over to the World of Spirit.

With the assistance of Your Children in Spirit, it is my passion to promote the expansion of our consciousness about the continuity of life, and the laws of nature, so that you may begin to heal and discover greater depths of contentment, joy and peace.

Everything in our universe is energy (including your thoughts, emotions, feelings and beliefs). Imagine your unlimited potential to have all this energy expanding, creating, healing and growing when you truly believe in yourself. Miracles are possible! Conveniently, freely, daily, possible!

The healing that comes from this book is of your own making. You, and only you, can decide to heal yourself and then put into action your healing process. Your logical mind will try to tell you otherwise but, the truth of the matter is, the only thing that can ever separate you from Your Child: is your mind.

The chattering, doubtful mind is negative energy from the ego, an aspect of yourself that can separate you from all creation. The ego-mind compares, judges and limits all aspects of love. The ego-mind will try to convince us that if our child is not physically present then we should be in constant pain and suffering. Remember: 'Pain is inevitable. Suffering is optional.' An ego denies you the eternal connection of love that exists between you and Your Child. The earth-bound ego erases all the joy and goodness that you shared with Your Child.

In contrast, your loving, heavenly heart is a much more powerful energy center, within you, that creates, nurtures, stores and promotes the higher vibration of love. When we choose to use our non-'second-guessing' heart to guide us through this journey of life, we find that we will truly discover peace and joy.

The choice is yours; you may love Your Child for all eternity, through your heart, or you may deny your connection through the fears of your ego-mind. My hope is that this book will assist you in choosing reward over loss; light over darkness; the continuity of life over death, and love over fear.

Love Your Child forever as they will love you! As Winnie the Pooh said, "If there ever comes a day when we can't be together, keep me in your heart, I'll stay forever." While hugs from Heaven may seem invisible…hugs from Heaven are real!

Chapter 1

The Fairy Tale of Death

"I know you
I walked with you once upon a dream
I know you
The gleam in your eyes is a familiar gleam
Yes, I know it's true
That visions are seldom all they seem.
But if I know you, I know what you'll do
You'll love me at once
The way you did once upon a dream."

– Lyrics from Walt Disney's movie Sleeping Beauty,
"Once Upon a Dream"

Death is but a fairy tale.

In the story of Sleeping Beauty, Princess Aurora pricks her finger on a spinning wheel spindle that has been cursed with a wicked spell by an angry witch. Aurora falls into a sleep that *appears* deathlike, but she only awaits to be awakened by "Love's True Kiss." The operative word is "appears" and death is a mere "appearance". "Not in death, but just a spell, this fateful prophecy you'll keep. And from this slumber you shall wake…..For love conquers all."

The love of Your Child can also conquer all, even their own death. Your Child is not dead. His or her consciousness is very much alive, and will live 'happily ever after'.

Death has always fascinated me. My first exposure to a human death was my great-grandfather, Alexander. When I was age nine, everyone said to me, "Doesn't he look so nice just sleeping up there in his casket?" But I thought, "How can he be just sleeping?" Where was the warm, expressive, funny personality of the man that I knew so well?

As a curious boy, I used to collect dead animals in my neighborhood; turtles, birds, fish and squirrels so that I, like a young Da Vinci, could study them up close and try to figure out why they no longer responded, breathed, or moved (like my lifeless grandpa). Out of respect for the animals, I would bury them in the backyard after my studies. From time to time, I would later dig up the carcasses to see if they were still there. My priest used to say, "From dust to dust," and, through the process of decomposition, I was starting to get it. My youthful studies, however, only resulted in more and more questions. 'What is death?'

In grade school, as an altar boy, I used to love receiving notices that I would be released early from school to serve at a funeral. I wanted to get as close to death as possible so that I could better understand it.

What was that body doing just lying there? Where had the Life Force gone, the soul? Why were the dead relatives so sad (if they believed in God, angels, heaven, eternity and all that stuff)?

My search for understanding death, and therefore life, continued throughout my teens, and still in my twenties as I pursued my bachelor's degree in Biology. I figured that I could study living things, on the cellular level, to get a better understanding of the Life Force.

Cells are very complicated and fascinating little energy changing systems. Cells convert energy, use energy, and create more cells like little Life Factories.

Perhaps I was onto something. But a very important experience happened to me my last year of college, one that would change me forever.

I was asked to join my premedical classmates in preparing a cadaver for the next term Anatomy Class. I agreed to help them because I felt it would give me more insight into understanding the physical aspect of my personal being. I will never forget "the body" being wheeled into the room (a 280 pound, 5'6" female, 40 years of age, who had died from cardiac arrest).

My friends and I had many great discussions on the subject of death that week while working on the cadaver. My biology book defined death as, "…the permanent termination of the biological functions that define a living organism." Clinically our professor told us that death is defined as the cessation of respiratory, cardio-vascular and brain functions. If someone relied on any machines to maintain these functions, then I guessed that they were still considered "alive"(at least, mechanically, but "What about alive fully?").

Working on the cadaver was amazing! To hold a human heart, the center of our feelings, in my hands, and feel, and see with my own eyes, that it really exists, was astounding.

The human brain, an organ unmatched by anything man could create, with all its grooves and valleys, (with its center of logic, analysis and cognitive thought) was a three dimensional miracle that I held in my hands.

But what about the 'organ' called the soul? I knew souls were not in my anatomy book, but there had to be 'such an organ', something physical that I could feel and see, something associated with the soul.

To my disappointment there was not such an organ. So how can "the body," lying in front of me, no longer sustain life if it still had all its organs, chemicals and cells which it had while still alive? Where was the energy, Life Force, or Soul? Perhaps "the body" is just a shell to temporarily hold and maintain the soul, in order for our souls to have a physical experience? Imagine – I was given the opportunity to experience it for real, not just to read about it in a textbook!

My quest for the Life Force continued in graduate school, as I decided to pursue the study of life on an even smaller level – *Molecular Biology*!

I wanted to understand how life functioned on a smaller degree within our bodies. Was there something in the DNA, RNA, or proteins that could help me understand the Soul, the Spirit or some Life Force?

An important law of nature tells us that, in biological systems, the structure of things determines their function. But, ultimately, I always came back to the concept and the word "energy", whether studying the body, a cell, or DNA. So our physical body is composed of organs (which are energy), cells (which are energy), and molecules which, too, are energy.

But my greatest lesson in graduate school did not come from within the lecture halls or the laboratories – rather it came from a child! As a graduate student at Roswell Cancer Institute, I had to complete service hours as part of my academic program. My friends all chose jobs that included reading to older patients, or running errands for family members of cancer patients.

My affinity was to work with children (since I thought that they would be fun, easy, and I could play during my service hours). My assignment was with Elizabeth, a beautiful nine year old girl with blonde locks, confident blue eyes, and a smile that warmed my heart. She was a leukemia patient who had spent several months at the institute getting radiation and chemotherapy. Elizabeth wanted to play the board game 'Candy Land' and I agreed. As I got lost in Lollipop Woods, and then got stuck in Molasses Swamp, Elizabeth made her way to Candy Castle (winning the game!). To my surprise, Elizabeth asked me why I was afraid of her. Nervously, I said that I was not afraid (but she knew better). She told me that all the older people were 'afraid' of her because she was dying.

With a deep gulp, and a panicked look on my face, she assured me with her grin, that I should not be afraid of her because she was going to heaven, and she was going to get to take better care of her mom, dad and little brother.

I was shocked at the candor that her little soul possessed. How could she even smile with the pain and suffering she had been experiencing, and knowing, too, that death was right around the corner?

I wished her a good day and hurried on to my test tubes and bacteria, for they didn't bother to challenge me with such strong emotions.

The next week, I returned for my service duty and found Elizabeth waiting for me as if she knew when I was coming back. This time she had 'The Game of Life' in front of her and somehow I knew this was not by chance.

With another angelic smile she told me it was my spin at life. All the numerous times that I played her game, with its 'new children', pay days, 'family trips', and taxes due on our journey to 'Millionaire Estates', she still sensed my underlying fear of her death, this nine year old girl. I did not know what lighthearted things to say, and I had trouble looking her in the eye. She spoke freely throughout the game about climbing over rainbows, finger painting the sky with God at sunset, singing with angels and dancing a polka with grandpa in heaven. I could only respond with a half smile and a nod. She was so sure, so at peace with her situation, and knew without a doubt that these things would come to be. She asked me if I believed her, and I said, with a whisper, "Yes".

"Really?" She then said that I was the first adult to believe her, and somehow I then felt like Elizabeth herself, as if I were totally convinced, too!

Her greatest concern was for her mom and dad. She explained that they were so sad, and that she did not want them to hurt so much. She asked me the most difficult question of my graduate program, "How can I make sure Mom and Dad understand?" I told her to tell them what she told me, and show them with the same persuasive smile. We hugged, and I went on my way to play the real game of life.

The following week I came to play with Elizabeth again but she was not at the usual table.

One of the nurses came over to tell me that Elizabeth had passed that Tuesday, with both the smile and the faith of an angel. The tears of this twenty-three year old could not be held back. I wept, not so much for Elizabeth, rather my tears were for me, because I had so much to learn, much trust to gain, and so far to grow. I was so overwhelmed that this little soul taught me so much about life over the competitive cardboard playing fields of 'Candy Land' and 'The Game of Life'. She had shown, by example, the most significant lesson of my graduate program!

The Universe provided me with more opportunities to work with children upon completing my graduate degree. My first job, out of graduate school, was at Children's Hospital in Buffalo, New York. I had the unique experience of working as a laboratory technician in one of the first *in vitro* fertilization clinics in the United States. I assisted in helping to make new babies in test tubes, new life. It was such a joy to witness how a new mom gets her chance to have a child of her own.

But, again, the questions started with how can uniting an egg and a sperm result in a little person? When does the soul, or Life Force, enter into this earthly plane? Again I found myself drawn to the children of the hospital by volunteering my time with terminally-ill children. Although my tenure was brief, there was much to learn from these children as they prepared to cross over into the World of Spirit. Each and every one of them was quite sure about the positive aspect of death, the continuity of life, and that there would be no separation from those they loved! Each child was certain of their role in helping those they would temporarily leave behind here on the physical lane. Perhaps, when Jesus said, "Unless you become as a little child, you cannot enter the kingdom of heaven," this is exactly what He meant. Kids get it, why don't we as adults? Should Heaven be any harder to attain for us than an Adult Ticket to Disneyland?

As a college Anatomy and Physiology instructor, the very first question I would pose to my classes was, "Define Life". Since it was a biology class, many students initially opted for the clinical answer (dealing with the basic functions of a living organism in defining life). But the discussion would get very interesting when students integrated their religious, family values, and cultural experiences into the Life Discussion. Words like 'Holy Spirit', 'Spirit' and 'Soul' were often used to discuss the Life Force. I would assign students their first project, to define the life force, and ultimately, no matter what belief systems students accepted, they invariably defined life as 'an energy force with a consciousness'.

My educational experience was most challenging, as were my days, (and too many nights!!!) as a Dean of Student Services. I was so protected and insolated in the intellectual world of academia, I did not ever imagine that I would have to deal with death so literally and emotionally.

I was faced with explaining death to many parents who lost their children while their sons and daughters were attending college. It was the most enlightening experience in my academic experience as Dean, because I was able to use my intuitive abilities to help a parent heal through the passing of their college-age child.

I found myself becoming a student of emotional intelligence and life long wisdom, as I was being taught with the assistance of my Spirit Guides and Angels. Never had I witnessed such grief and pain than when I had to tell a parent that their child had passed. I wanted so badly to tell them about the World of Spirit and the continuity of life, but that explanatory moment would have to wait until this book came into being. It occurred to me that my life's mission was to help understand the process of death, the meaning of the physical life, and the continuity of life after this mortal experience.

Then there were religions' questions about Life and the Soul. I was raised as a "true" Catholic (baptized and confirmed, and an altar boy of seven years). I will never forget how exciting it was to learn about the dinosaurs in second grade. In Religious Education class, that same year, we learned about creationism's Adam and

Eve. When I asked Sister Mary Margaret what came first, Adam and Eve, or the dinosaurs, she replied that dinosaurs did not exist, and that their fossils were placed in the earth, by the devil, to divert us from believing in God. Of course, I had to stand in the corner because I was not acting the part of an unquestioning or obedient sheep.

One other time, in Catechism Class, I asked how Christ could ascend if Isaac Newton's Law of Gravity were real. The classroom's corner became a welcoming place for me during my parochial education.

But I was to learn more about God, and the universe, through my many walks and meditations in nature. It is Natural Law that defines the essence of my beliefs. Nature speaks to me in so many ways and always shows me the truth. The trepidation of swimming upstream, instead of allowing the flow to take you in its desired direction, rewards us by presenting us with the cycles of physical life. The cycles of physical life through the seasons: the stillness and tranquility of a tree, the joyful expression of a blossomed rose, the transformation of a caterpillar into a butterfly, the gentleness of a breeze, and the purification caused by a hard summer rain.

Buddhists, and other religions adherents, believe that death occurs when the consciousness finally leaves the body to go on to the next life. Through intuition, and the channeling of wisdom from many great masters, I believe that death is the cessation of the connection between our mind (or consciousness) and the physical body. Our human body is of a lower vibration and disintegrates at death because it needs energy to maintain its earthly organization. The mind is not a physical thing; rather it is of a higher vibration and is a formless continuum that has no beginning and no end.

Your Child's consciousness lives eternally beyond the death of their physical body. Their physical body was just a temporary 'balloon' in which they were a guest. Their consciousness is the air within that balloon that is released, and integrated once again with the Universe.

One thing is for sure; Life is eternal and has no opposite. Death is the opposite of birth, and both are natural processes.

Death of Your Child's physical body is simply the birth of their soul into the complete and full World of Spirit. In fact, many times, in readings, Your Child will come through to ask that you celebrate *both* their birthday into the physical world and their birthday into the World of Spirit. After all, "Isn't it always better to have more opportunities for cake and ice cream with two 'birthday' celebrations a year?"!

As Your Child's physical body sleeps, their consciousness begins a new adventure beyond anything you can imagine (from any fairytale you were ever told). Your love will always awaken your sleeping beauty from his or her slumber, and they will live, and rejoice, happily ever after.

Chapter 2

The Field of Wonderland

"Children yet, the tale to hear,
Eager eye and willing ear,
Lovingly shall nestle near.
In a Wonderland they lie,
Dreaming as the days go by,
Dreaming as the summers die:
Ever drifting down the stream –
Lingering in the golden gleam –
Life, what is it but a dream?"

– *Alice in Wonderland by Lewis Carroll*

In Lewis Carroll's story of *Alice in Wonderland*, Alice is exposed to the ridiculous social rules that are blindly accepted by society. Alice is asked to give away her unique gift – the unique gift – of any child, her innocent non-prejudice in order to survive in the world of adults.

It is essential for you to remove the belief systems you are borrowing from our present day society, and to 'go within' to fully comprehend and understand the concepts presented in this book. It is time to leave the illusions of the world with the world and to recognize the truths within the 'Looking Glass' of your soul.

Everything in the universe is energy! This one sentence says it all, pure and simple - just as a child. Every thought, feeling, belief, attitude and experience that you have created in your life is energy. The universe is a dynamic web of interconnected energy called "the field" or 'the mind of God'.

Einstein said, "The field is the only reality." Everything is composed of energy and energy vibrates with various frequencies; it moves and dances to a Universal Pulse. Lower vibrations of energy are what you and I perceive as solid objects in the physical plane of existence, while higher vibrations are phenomenon, experienced through an invisible reality of the World of Spirit.

An old way of thinking of the physical universe was that everything was composed of independent little units of matter. We were thought to be disconnected beings of matter separated from "the source" of God. Newton described a world, his world, in which matter follows specific laws of motion through space and time. But physics and metaphysics define even the tiniest bits of matter as energy, and Quantum Physics states that all bits of matter are linked with everything else.

We humans are packages of quantum energy who constantly exchange information with the inexhaustible field of energy. We are all connected to one another, and we are all part of the Universal Life Force called the 'collective consciousness', God Force, or Holy Spirit.

Wow! You see, you are truly eternal and infinite, when you realize you are part of the God Force. Can you say that out loud now, even as you silently read this? "I am truly eternal and infinite."

Everything in the universe pulsates with energy and all energy contains information. You are an informational energy pattern that emits energy into the Universe through your consciousness (which, in and of itself, is a powerful energy field).

You have an eternal and evolving memory of energy, and you leave your energy fingerprints upon every relationship and situation you have ever experienced. Likewise, Your Child, then, is energy that is eternal, immortal, and is bonded to all there is (including you).

Your Child also has left energy fingerprints (like those expressive finger paintings they created) on all that they encountered, accomplished and believed in while they shared this physical plane with you.

For example, Bill was a bright and intelligent fourth grader who had a desire to design buildings by drawing them, and then by building the structures with his set of Legos. From the World of Spirit, his soul maintained his love of architecture, and during a reading to his mother, I could hear and feel Bill's love for his Lego buildings.

A deceased teenager, named Jillian, gave one of her greatest gifts to her parents, during a reading, when she communicated how she helped raise monies for medical supplies for the children of Africa, and then visited the country for her college summer break to provide community service. Eternal energy fingerprints from the unseen World of Spirit are eternally available for all to see, and feel, and are shared in readings with Your Children in Spirit.

Many compare energy to God, for energy is boundless, limitless, continuous, miraculous, pure and omnipotent. The Field is an intimately interconnected field of energy and everything in the universe, from Your Child's body, their thoughts and feelings, are all part of it. To paraphrase Einstein, "Energy can neither be created or destroyed".

Energy cannot be created or destroyed; it is eternal. Your Child is pure energy (I bet you all have stories of their boundless creative energy!), so all of energy's principles and characteristics apply to them!

Imagine that Your Child is every thought, every dream, every feeling that they have ever experienced, and you were responsible for creating many of their wonderful celebrations, holidays and magical moments that abounded in their awareness. The memories, thoughts and feelings you shared together are still everlasting for, energetically, they are part of your soul and theirs. The consciousness of Your Child exists with no limitations.

Sam conveyed to me, during a reading from the World of Spirit, his last "physical" Christmas he shared with his father, as they played all afternoon with his Matchbox race track under the Christmas tree. His memories, of this wonderful gift of sharing and exchanging fun and laughter with his father, are still with him as Energy fingerprints of a beautiful Christmas memory. It was the best possible gift that Sam's father could ever wish for. The only limitation of Your Child in Spirit is their physical aspect, not their reality.

The amount of energy in the universe is stable, but the vibration of energy can be transformed to a higher, or lower, vibration. You are an energy transformer, and, through your consciousness, you can create the high vibrations of

joyful love (or the lower vibrations of paralyz-
ing fear). All your experiences are energy, and
how you react and respond to everything is also
energy. You have the free will to respond with
a multitude of vibrations, like the many shades
of color in a king-sized box of crayons. You can
choose to color your world today with the blues,
or the radiance of reds, oranges and yellows.

For example, Marcie presented a comforting message to her mother through the image
of a bluebird swimming in the birdbath during
a reading. Marcie wanted her mom to know
how she saw her mother spending hours in the
backyard, watching bluebirds. Her mother felt
the warm loving thoughts, from her daughter
in spirit, but rather chose to express a lower vibration (of pain and suffering). Stewart, on the
other hand, transformed a father's love from
his son (Stewy, Jr.) into the higher vibration of
appreciation and gratitude when Stewy, Jr. presented himself through the feelings they shared
in the family garage while fixing things.

As a parent, Your Child in Spirit will ask that
you transform their love into more love to be
shared with others. In Spirit, children realize
the perpetual expression of love is like a toy top

that spins and spins with joy, for all to enjoy its centrifugal dance.

Children that have passed will often express the miracle of lives shared and their appreciation for the gifts shared while on the physical plane. This is part of their eternal energy and, as a fun movie, they like to replay it over and over and share the vibration of laughter. Your Child in Spirit is at a higher vibration, and it is through this elevated vibration that you can better connect with Your Child in Spirit. The higher your consciousness expresses a vibration of love, compassion, and gratitude, the easier it is for you to feel their presence in Spirit. As a boy named Charles once put it, in a reading, "Dad, isn't it easier to catch a pop fly with a glove than with your bare hands? Protect yourself with the vibration of love, and reach for the stars!" Based on Charles' analysis, we need the insulation-and-the-comfort of love to ease the sting of catching "death"; of catching the 'pop flies' that life throws at us.

Energy vibrates and moves with various frequencies and speeds. Slow moving energy is dense, and exists in a physical form as a solid, liquid, or a gas. Your Child temporarily lived in a physical world, within a physical body, with energy that vibrates slowly.

Think of Your Child's Teddy bear, a physical piece of cloth and stuffing. The real, meaningful portion of Your Child's Teddy bear is the love that Your Child carried in their heart for it. The bear is but a toy, used for Your Child to create, feel and express love and affection. Your Child's own body is similar to the Teddy bear as it is a temporary shell to house a soul (a special soul to you). Again, the slower the vibration, the denser the physical form of energy...children are slow, Teddy bears are even slower.

The World of Spirit is part of the Universe but it is different from the physical world that we now reside in. In the World of Spirit, where Your Child now resides, there are no time-and-space-dimension-limitations that we have here in the physical world. Your Child can experience things very quickly, with many individuals (simultaneously) and Your Child can be at many places, at the same time, because his/her soul has so many dimensions.

Maggie was excited to let her mom and dad know that she was with them both even though her parents lived apart. She presented information, during the reading, to let them know that her energy could be in more than one place at a time, and that this was a fun and adventurous part of being a Spirit. Your Child's Spirit can show you things that have happened in the past and give you ideas about some likely outcomes for future events. As an example, Ray's mom was concerned about what happened when her son's body was found (under a rock in a remote dirt road). Ray came through to acknowledge that he had a 'spell' or seizure that disoriented him and that he lost his direction. Ray was able to show me his passing. He left his car, and wandered off, and found a large rock to shade himself from the sun. Ray passed away peacefully in his sleep, from dehydration and sunstroke.

Andy came through, in another reading for his mom, to show her a special gift that he had in-store for her birthday, which was several days away from the reading. He wanted her to go to church. She hadn't left the house much, since his passing, but decided to listen to her son's message. To her surprise, on her birthday, the pastor of her church read a poem that Andy had written for his mom when he was a young boy for Mother's Day.

Again, Andy is an example of how Your Children in Spirit can show you events to come, or, at least, give us a hint of what is to come. Sometimes Your Child just can't help not keep a secret (as they find it hard to conceal exciting news here in the physical world).

Debbie came for a reading and her daughter told her of a big surprise party, in the coming month of July, and that *yellow roses* were going to be presented to her! Debbie thought that the message could not be right but, Debbie was not so surprised to find a family reunion on her birthday and, sure enough, she received *yellow roses* from her mother (and her daughter in spirit!).

So you see that Your Child in Spirit has a unique advantage of living outside the constraints of time and space. They can 'see the image of the puzzle' before 'all the pieces' are put together, they can ride on the teeter-totter and sit on the swing simultaneously. The World of Spirit is a magical place, truly a wonderland!

You are the architect of your own reality and you do so through a Universal participatory process. Your consciousness influences energy (the stuff that everything is made of) and directly affects the energy of the Universe. Image energy is like Silly Putty (I was told by a Child in Spirit) – think of all the shapes you can form! You craft your own reality through your beliefs, and Your Child in Spirit understands this very well, and wants for you to embrace this idea so that you can continue to co-create miracles together.

We live in an interactive reality where we change the world around us by changing what happens inside of us with our thoughts, emotions, feelings and our beliefs. So, your world is nothing more than a reflection of what you accept as your beliefs, and you have the power to choose your beliefs. Beliefs are the combined forces of what you think in your mind and what you feel in your heart. Beliefs carry all the power to create your reality. You can choose to think of yourself as a little energy transmitter in the vast universe of abundant energy. You transmit signals through your thoughts, beliefs, responses and attitudes. Similar forms of energy attract similar forms of energy. If you transmit 'vanilla' then the Universe will *not* provide you with 'strawberry' or 'chocolate', you get only 'vanilla'. See how great Your Child in Spirit is at making (what we think – is only a complicated sticky mess) into a tasty dessert? It is so important to play in the Heavens of After Death—for there is no After Life: Life always is!

I bring the topic of belief to your attention at this time to prepare your mind and heart to accept the continuity of life. On a child's circular, model train track, the train continues to go around and around. Your Son or Daughter is eternal, and your connection is permanent, if you believe and stay on that track. Their continued playful participation in your life will be possible if you open your heart and mind to the belief of their presence. Listen to them 'whistle' to you as they let you know that they are riding along life with you! What a wonderful belief to accept, and surrender to, and merrily take a ride on the Eternal Express. My favorite Christmas story is *The Polar Express* in which a little boy is asked to "believe" and, in believing, he can hear the higher vibration of love. If you, too, believe, then you can hear Your Child in Spirit!

There is an interesting concept known as Entanglement - it means that things which had been connected physically, and then were separated, act as if they are still linked. Objects can be unlinked but instantaneously influence one another, no matter how far apart they are. Scientists have found enough evidence to suggest that this Entanglement action may work beyond the grave, with its effect felt after the link between objects is broken. Subatomic particles to stars, demonstrate this principle of *interconnectiveness*. So imagine that Your Child is entangled with you forever. Every moment, every emotion, every experience with Your Child, is entangled with your energy forever; there are no boundaries or barriers to the principle of Entanglement. It's like a joyful "wrestling match" on the carpet, the front lawn, in snowbanks or the surf or pool. Children from Spirit often relay messages of what may seem as ordinary, every day moments: the baloney sandwich, the walk to the bus, the red wagon, stories on the front porch, laughing at grandpa's jokes or playing house, and these memories are entangled with them as part of their eternal vibration.

Mitchell spoke to me from spirit to give his parents a message about the night they all went to the Griffith Observatory to witness the rings of Saturn, the red star Mars, and a large nebula near Aquarius. He said, as they shared the heavens on that night, they will continue to share the heavens forever, entangled as stardust from the depths of the Universe.

Most likely you have walls of photographs, photo albums, or videos of colorful moments of magical times shared with Your Child. Symbolically, these are similar to the treasured vibrations Entangled in your energy forever. These pictures are snapshots of special moments in the gallery of your life. All that you and Your Child have shared and created are vibrations entangled in "the field", the eternal wonderland that we call heaven (or home).

Chapter 3

The Anatomy of a Kid

"Snips and snails, and puppy dog tails
That's what little boys are made of.
Sugar and spice and everything nice
That's what little girls are made of."

– *Old English Nursery Rhyme, Mother Goose*

The body of Your Child consists of more than just bones, muscles and blood.

The human body can be thought of as a 'field of energy' with different levels of consciousness, in parallel planes, that inter-penetrate each other. It is kind of like multicolored cotton candy; the physical body is the paper holder, the soul is the 'spun sugar', and the candy's multicolors represent the various vibrations of energy around the body.

The physical aspect of the body vibrates at the lowest frequencies of energy. Your Child's physical body is energy, and bodies require energy to maintain their high degree of bodily order. Although the physical body seems solid, scientists have discovered that the human body is mostly an empty space. In fact, the Universe appears to be mostly empty space, and scientists call it 'the Zero Field' and it is actually NOT empty: it contains lots of energy!

Your physical senses perceive the physical world as a "solid only" because your visual senses cannot discern the 'dancing light' that you and Your Child really are. Your Child is made of the same stuff that the stars are made of; stardust and light! Science can dissect and categorize Your Child's body into a general hierarchy as follows: *atoms* (atomic energy), *molecules* (molecular energy), *cells* (cellular energy), *tissues* (mechanical, chemical, electrical energy), *organs* (mechanical, chemical, electrical energy), *organ systems* (mechanical, chemical, electrical energy) and then *the body* (mechanical, chemical, electrical energy).

Every level of Your Child's biology requires energy to maintain a highly detailed and specific organizational structure, and the structure is required so that the proper function can be performed to sustain life while Your Child's soul is temporarily housed inside. Your Child's physical body provides a stable and solid foundation for the other energy bodies that surround it (similar to how their skeleton provides an established support system for the other tissues of their body). When Your Child is within his/her physical body, their body allows them to experience the pure illusion of separation (as you are experiencing now in your body). In order for Your Child to clarify his/her personal character and accomplish his/her Soul Mission or Purpose of Growth (and development of this lifetime) the essence of their individuality is expressed in the physical. Like a great magician who hides the rabbit in his hat, Your Child's physical body ("The Hat") is separated from knowing their animated soul body (The "Living Rabbit"); this is "Life's" great trickery. This is important because Your Child would not have any enriching emotional, physical, intellectual and spiritual experiences if they knew why they were here and what they were supposed to be and do. It is through the experiences of their life, with you in the physical world, that separates the knowing within their soul, and that is how the magic of discovering, expanding, developing and healing happens (remember: the separation of the physical body is just an illusion, it is not real!).

The physical body contains the five physical senses of sight, sound, taste, touch and hearing so that Your Child can perceive and react to his/her physical environment. Many times we believe, or should I say, "Our Egos want us to believe", that if our physical senses cannot perceive something then: it is not real. As Einstein said, "Not everything that can be counted, matters. And not everything that matters – can be counted."!

But just because you cannot see something, or someone, does not mean that it is not or they are not there. We cannot see electricity, atoms or radio waves but we have created devices that can see beyond our own abilities! Imagine all that we have invented to expand our vision - microscopes and telescopes, CT scans, MRI's and X-rays! Can you see atoms? Can you see microwaves? This brings a new level of awareness for that not-so-imaginary friend Your Child had while here on this earth plane. Science and metaphysics complement each other in recognizing and accepting the World of the Unseen.

Within the World of Spirit, energy vibrates at a faster rate of speed, many times faster outside the normal range of what our usual senses can detect. Your intuitive abilities will allow you to effectively connect with Your Child in Spirit. It will be important for you to explore the type of intuition you possess so that you can establish an effective communication system with Your Child in Spirit.

Your Child's physical body was surrounded by an aura, or Field of Energy that extends as far as their outstretched arms can reach and, at least, the full length of their body (when they were in their physical bodies). This Energy Field can be thought of as an information center of all their emotions, attitudes, beliefs, thoughts, experiences and ideas when they were in their physical body and it survives the death of the physical body! This will be a major means of communication with your son or daughter in the World of Spirit to be discussed in this volume.

Their aura was also a Highly Sensitive Perceptual System that allowed Your Child to interact and respond to their external environment while they were here in the physical plane. When Your Child was in his/her physical body, he or she was constantly in communication with everything and everyone around them through this electromagnetic field of energy (transmitting and receiving signals and signs). In fact, this is the means of how Your Child interacted and played with the energy in "The Field" that comprises our Universe. Most of the information we receive about people, places, experiences and things is found in the energy field that surrounds those persons and events. Every time Your Child wanted to play a new game, draw a picture, learn a new skill, develop a feeling about someone, analyze a new concept, discover a new belief, they generated energy within their aura. It is by these messages (from within the Energy Field of Your Child) that your *intuition* can perceive, and assimilate, your deceased progeny because this energy exists beyond the death of the physical body. When Your Child was in their physical body, they did not have to stand in front of you in order for you to feel love for them. Right? They could have been at school or visiting grandma, hundreds of miles away, and you still felt the same loving energy for them. The same applies to when Your Child is in Spirit; your love still has no boundaries!

When Your Child was in their physical body they were surrounded immediately with the energy of their etheric body. The etheric body is a subtle body that is the mirror image of Your Child's physical body and contains all information (i.e., energy). It is a hologram; every part of the etheric body contains the whole (just as every cell in the physical body contains the same genetic DNA material to express any type of cell within the body). The etheric body gave vitality, health, life and organization to Your Child's physical body. It attuned their consciousness to the principle of Energy, and contains seven major energy centers (called chakras) and numerous energy channels (called meridians). Your Child's etheric body has the ability to generate energy of many frequencies (remember the colors of cotton candy?). By measuring the vibration of the chakras (the body's energy centers), we can determine Your Child's overall long-term and current life issues. Chakras are spinning wheels of light, vortices (or funnels) of energy that are configured in the structure of Your Child's Energy Field. Your Child's consciousness is part of the energy field, and it moves from one vibrating frequency to the next, and such energy flows to all parts of their body.

The seven chakras are aligned in an ascending column from the base of the spine to the top of the head. Each chakra has specific archetypes associated with it and each level has universally the same emotional qualities (that come from the core human experience and represent the positive and negative qualities within us). The chakras can be thought of as the energy connection between the physical world and the world of the non-physical or Spirit. Any area of their body that does not transmit at its normal frequency indicates a 'dis-ease'. It is important for you to learn about the chakra system so that you can better understand yourself as an Energy Field, maintain optimum health, and know how to best connect with Your Guides and Children in Spirit.

The astral body, sometimes referred to as the emotional body, is the next plane of existence of Your Child's total body. This aspect of their body exists in the vibration of the astral plane (or in the dream state) where time does not exist and where experience is driven by their emotions, passions and desires. It is thought to be the plane which bridges our physical brains and the Higher Level Mind. Scientists now realize what metaphysicians have known for many years, that Your Child's mind is not confined to their brain. Their mind extends in all directions and dimensions with every thought, feeling, idea and belief they have ever created. That makes Your Little Kid: very, very big, considering energy travels at least at the speed of light! Your Child's dreams exist in this realm of the Universe, and you have the ability to connect with them, in the astral plane. In fact, many times when a parent has difficulty connecting to Their Child, during their day-to-day communications (and Your Child in spirit always communicates with you everyday!), then children easily come through in their dreams.

When you carry the lowering energies of fear and grief it becomes more difficult for you to connect with Your Child in the higher vibration of Spirit. During sleep, you can enter into the higher vibration of the astral plane and connect with Your Child in Spirit.

The astral body gives Your Child the ability to have desires, emotions, and imagination. It also allows for Your Child to have his/her psychic abilities so that they can connect with other family members (and friends in spirit) and with you in the physical plane. It includes a full range of emotions ranging from: fear, hate, and sorrow – to love, happiness and even ecstasy.

Once I did a reading for a mom. Her daughter, Trish, came through by identifying herself with her desire for riding horses. Her blissful energy was so strong when she thought of her horses. Trish provided detailed descriptions about horses including their Granny Apple treats, their handmade blankets, and their sneezing fits whenever roses were present.

Additionally, we are emotional beings, and this level of emotive existence is very easy to feel when a medium does a reading that connects you with Your Child in Spirit. Your Child's emotional energy (of all their lifetime experiences) is carried at this vibration in the astral, and this emotional energy influences their physical body. Our Children's bodies are walking bibliographies of everything they have experienced; especially emotionally. When Your Child harbors an emotion in his/her body, it can also be felt even when they are in spirit.

Johnny had a great love for his younger brother, Nathan, whom he held as a strong green vibration in his heart. During a reading, Johnny's feelings were overwhelming, and could be sensed so clearly in my own heart, as he conveyed to his parents the intensity of this love that he had for the grief-stricken little brother. Johnny communicated to his parents the affection he and his brother shared when they played one-on-one basketball in the driveway, video games on their computers, and when they ate pizza on Friday nights.

The aspect of Your Child, that allows awareness of meaning and exists outside the dimensions of both time and space, is called the mental body (or intellectual body). This higher level of existence facilitates cognition and knowing and gives Your Child the ability to discern and to have thoughts, beliefs, concepts and higher psychic abilities. Your Child's mental consciousness, ranging from judgment, mental fear and depression to compassion, peace, awe and joy, is housed here. Many times when a child had depression, or a great fear, they provided this information in a reading; mainly to convey to their parents that they had conquered it.

Jackie suffered from years of depression because she feared that no one liked her. Her mother tried, in so many ways, to connect Jackie with counselors and to get her involved in school activities. Jackie was overcome by her depression and took her own life. It was important to let Jackie's mom know, during the reading, that Jackie's own thoughts were responsible for her fears, and no matter what Mom did to try to eliminate the fears, to help Jackie heal: Jackie could not release her dark feelings. Jackie wore a large red "R" on her chest, as so many children do that have taken *Responsibility* for their own passing.

Many times children will speak as to how their powerful and creative minds influenced their willpower to make choices that were not fear-based. The physical plane contains so many fears, and it is important to remind our children that fears are not a place from which to create, build and grow. You can help guide Your Child from fear, but you cannot regulate or control the fear that is embedded in their mind.

Kevin expressed his fear of everything, from diseases to people, in his reading to his father. He was so unhappy with life that he did not have the desire to live. He was thankful that Dad provided him an excellent college education, a stable home, many loving memories, but Kevin's ego ruled his mind, and no matter how many talks and how many professional counselors Dad provided, Kevin could not overcome the influence of his mind. He took his own life, and wanted Dad to forgive himself, and to stop asking, 'Why?'. Kevin worked with his father to help him heal his mind and, in effect, helped heal Kevin's own mind now in Spirit.

The most pleasant part of readings comes from feeling the joy and compassion that a child has for a loved one. The mental body contains the energy of the high vibration of compassion and empathy. When a child experiences a long-term disease, and their parents have to endure the pain of seeing them suffer and hurt, it is very difficult for the child. Often, during readings, children communicate with great passion as to how much they appreciated Mom and Dad stroking their hair, humming a song, offering encouraging smiles, kissing their foreheads and comforting them when feeling upset.

Mary Ann came for a reading and learned that her daughter, Sara, was so happy with her mom, who was an art teacher. Mary Ann was helping children understand the importance of their own creative abilities, and how their imagination is a gift from God. Sara inspired her mom to produce a Butterfly Bush Project to celebrate life. Mary Ann greatly appreciated the care and inspiration from her little muse. All the thoughts and memories Your Child has of you and with you are an integral part of their energy field, and since energy is eternal, your connection to and with them is also eternal.

The highest level of Your Child is their Spiritual Body, sometimes called the Causal (or Soul) Body. This is the portion of Your Child that is pure energy, or God. This is the aspect of Your Child that lasts forever and is the depository for all consciousness and virtues cultivated by Your Child in each personal lifetime. It is a treasure chest that safekeeps all the willpower, wisdom and creative intelligence that Your Child has experienced in all lifetimes. Envision all of the riches and prizes that Your Child acquired and brought with them to heaven, on their most recent lifetime journey with you. What gifts did you offer to them so that they could bring these treasures to God? Perhaps, a trip to laugh at the monkeys in the zoo, a pony ride, a sand castle on the beach, coloring Easter eggs, or just eating homemade chocolate chip cookies. The causal body is the source of Your Child's personality, causing them to exist and just be. It is this energy that mediums connect with during a reading (and share with the parents the mission, goal or journey of their child's soul in the specific lifetime that was just experienced). Most importantly, though, it is vital for the child to communicate experiences from many other lifetimes to demonstrate to their parents that they are eternal, and they have experienced many lives aside from their shortened one. It always amazes me when a child comes through, during a reading, and explains how in a past life they might have been the parent, or sibling, to their parents. We all exchange roles: male/female, parent/child, clever/foolish, and affection/disgust, acquiring wisdom in our lifetimes so that we can become "Wholly" and more God-like.

Molly explained to her mother in a reading that, although her life was short this time in the physical world, she had acquired the skill of speaking her mind about her feelings. And her mom validated that Molly sure did speak her mind! For many lifetimes, Molly experienced lives in which she could not speak her mind (from being an Egyptian slave girl to an enlisted confederate soldier). She did not have the option to speak her truth. Molly acknowledged the love she had for her mom who provided Molly a comfortable home environment where she felt safe, freely expressing herself. It is through the many lifetime experiences, that Your Child experiences with you, that their soul becomes "wholly". Their treasure chest, of many lifetimes shared, is filled with the eternal wisdom and love that they carry in their causal body.

So, when your ego-mind tries to convince you that Your Child is no longer here, remember their energy body. An eternal electromagnetic field of abundant memories shared, thoughts exchanged, feelings disclosed, experiences revealed and love offered. You have access to their energy body forever and always.

Chapter 4

Peek-A-Boo I See You

"A whole new world
A new fantastic point of view
No one to tell us no
Or where to go
Or say we're only dreaming.
A whole new world
A dazzling place I never knew
But when I'm way up here
It's crystal clear
That now I'm in a whole new world with you."

— Lyrics from Walt Disney's movie Aladdin,
"A Whole New World"

As a medium, I have been blessed to experience the whole new World of Spirit. It is a fantastic point of view of our external existence. Through readings by a medium, Children in Spirit rejoice in this dazzling vibration and their enthusiasm, with their parents. A medium is a person who can hear, see and/or feel the presence of Spirit Guides or loved ones who have passed to the World of Spirit. Anyone can be a medium. In fact, we are all mediums in a way. Spirit shares a constant dialogue with you; it is just a matter of listening carefully, feeling Spirit's presence, and seeing the endless signs that the Spirit World gives to you.

The energy from the World of Spirit is very subtle, so it takes great concentration to be open and to allow the feelings, words, images or messages to come through. Spirit speaks in quiet and soft whispers, with great wisdom and compassion, and is often precise and succinct, and sometimes amazingly "humorous" (because

Spirit says things in a new light—a new way of "thinking").

Children are very open to communicating with their loved ones, (especially their parents) once they have crossed over. Almost always, Your Child in Spirit will want you to know that he/she is being taken care of with the guidance of grandparents, aunts, uncles, friends or other relatives from the Other Side. They want you to know that they are connected to your heart and there is truly no separation, ever. Remember that death is only an illusion of the mind on this earthly level, and Your Child in Spirit will do all he/she can to remind you of how truly close he/she is to you.

As far back as when I was in my crib, I remember awakening each morning to four beautiful Spirit Guides at my bedroom window. They told me that I was going to help people understand and see their (*Spirit's*) world – a world of peace, contentment and joy, a world free from fear and worries. They told me that I was going to "heal" people, in a very different way, and my method was going to be of my own creation. These Spirits let me know that they were my friends and more of them would guide me in my calling to help others throughout my life.

Children are so open to spirits but, as we grow older; we tend to negate and deny our connections to those who love and guide us by way of Spirit.

Throughout my life, various Spirit Guides have accompanied me to help me better understand their mystical language and how to engage them in discussions.

Our conversations are more telepathic, with fewer words but lots of pictures, signs, symbols and, most importantly, feelings. I can often hear them speak actual words to me, too. The type of mediumship that I will share with you is mental in nature. Mental mediumship is the form of communication in which the medium mentally hears, sees and feels messages from Spirit. During a reading, Your Child in Spirit can share images, symbols, feelings, sounds and words with me (or with my Spirit Guides) by imprinting them telepathically in my mind. Many times it is basically 'my people' (in Spirit) talking to 'your people' (in Spirit); something like ambassadors at a world conference, or emissaries at a high-level, United Nations' Summit. In contrast, there is also physical mediumship, in which Your Child in Spirit can manipulate energy here on this physical plane by manifesting perceptible noises, voices or by materializing objects.

There are three major types of mental mediumship that I commonly use to communicate with Your Child in Spirit: 1) clairvoyance, 2) clairaudience and 3) clairsentience.

Clairvoyance is a type of mediumship that involves clear seeing and refers to the power to see an event or an image in the past, present, or even the future. A clairvoyant has the ability to receive information in the form of visual symbols, signs or images. The 'third eye' or inner eye, located in the center of the forehead and associated with intuition, is the central 'lens' of clairvoyance. Spirits like to communicate many times using images, like the old saying goes, "A picture is worth a thousand words." A great deal of literal and symbolic information can be communicated through an image. Your Children will often choose objects important to them (or to you) and present a powerful and enriching message with many layers of meaning.

For example, I remember, during a reading, Tommy (a young man of twelve who passed several weeks after being hit in the head with a baseball) came through to his grief-stricken mom who had not smiled since his passing.

During the reading, he referred to a 'clown face with the smile' and associated it with his passing. Come to find out, there was the face of a clown painted over the hospital bed in the children's ward where Tommy eventually died. Tommy's "Headstone" (as it were) was a powerful message for his mother: because the clown had a big smile on its face, Tommy wanted his mom to smile again too! Tommy also showed me a connection to his dad and golfing. Dad was putting on the sixteenth green. Literally, the family lived on the sixteenth green, but the golf swing was a symbolic way for his dad to start enjoying life and playing as if his son were still with him.

Lena came for a reading to connect with her daughter, Susie. Susie provided imagines of turtles with bright colors and intricate patterns on their shells. Lena literally had just spent time in the Hawaiian Islands, as a healing trip to help overcome her grief, and Lena had been swimming with large sea turtles. Lena received a beautifully painted turtle, from a friend, just days before her reading. I believe that Susie wanted her mother to know that Susie was with her in Hawaii, and she wanted Mom to know that she was with Mom when Mom received the turtle gift. Symbolically, I also believe that Susie wanted her mom to 'come out of her shell' and move forward with her life, too.

Sara was amazed when she came for her reading because she kept seeing her daughter's favorite: Dragonflies! Everywhere she went, there were images of dragonflies and, during her reading, it was validated by her Daughter in Spirit that she was showing her dragonflies to let Sara know she was close by. Her daughter had painted images of dragonflies before she passed, and her mom had given her a dragon-fly pin, with which she was buried. Her daughter was also symbolically saying 'Be strong, and fly high with your thoughts'. It is amazing how carefully Your Child in Spirit chooses objects that *very clearly connect to you* on so many levels. Spirits are wise and choose their objects very specifically, correctly and conscientiously.

As a medium, I have developed a spiritual vocabulary with my Spirit Guides and Children in Spirit. Spirits know what certain images mean to me and can use them to convey messages, kind of like a code. It is important, during a reading, that I define what an object means to me, but I want to ensure there is an even bigger meaning to the person receiving the reading. Here's an example: you might literally love yellow roses, so Your Child provides yellow roses as symbols when they want to share their great appreciation to you for helping to serve others. A ship often symbolizes a career to me, a cake a birthday; rain means sorrow, an umbrella means protection, and a mirror means self-reflection (just to name a few).

I encourage parents to develop their own Spiritual Vocabulary with their children so that it makes communication easier for both parties. You can create a series of signs and symbols that have specific meaning to you and Your Child in Spirit, and Your Child will use them, from time to time, to let you know how close-by they are.

Once, during a reading, Joey (a teenager in Spirit) kept using images of fishing to communicate with his mom. My Spiritual Vocabulary for 'fishing' implies that Mom was searching (fishing) for a new way to think and believe spiritually. It also was carefully chosen at the time because Dad was on a fishing trip. Joey communicated further that he was with his favorite fisherman: his grandpa, on the other side. See how wise and clever Your Child in Spirit can be? They are masters at using just the right images to let you know they are still connected to you.

Betty received an image of a crosswalk from her son, George (and to me it meant, 'Walk her life path, within her beliefs and she would surely find her way across the Road of Life'). It also seems that Betty's son, George, painted crosswalks, as a summer job, and once got a J-walking ticket because he didn't stay inside the lines. Incredible! What a layered depth of symbolism!

A second method for communicating is clairaudience, which is clear hearing or the ability to obtain impressions of sound, voices or music that are not audible to normal hearing. Sometimes, Your Child in Spirit can speak through others in their real-life conversations, movies, music and any physical, auditory means to get their message to your ears! But, many times, your children will want to share a special song, saying, or sound that only you will specifically recognize.

We can hear with our spiritual ears and, many times, the messages will come through as whispers, laughter or crying. For many it is hard to know if clairaudience is true communication (versus hearing things in their head). Numerous parents ask me how do they know when they hear things, within their own head, if it is their own mind or Their Child who is actually speaking to them? I reply to them that they are to feel the voice and their heart will validate for them if it is Their Child.

Your Children in Spirit can speak to you through others, too. I was getting ready to do a reading one Saturday morning and, as I was jogging, I overheard a very brief description from two ladies power-walking saying, "...the green shirts." I knew, within my heart, this was information for a reading that day, and when the time came, I would feel who was to receive that precise message. Later that day, I met with a mom who just lost her son at school, and I mentioned the green shirts. Mom explained the entire school purchased green shirts to honor her son (Justin) who was killed while leaving school. Green was Justin's favorite color.

Once I was getting ready to do a reading and I kept hearing the song in my head, "You are My Sunshine" over and over. I accepted it as information for a reading. That evening I read for a mom and I felt the need to tell her about the song. It turns out it was her daughter's favorite song. Kelly sang it at a recital and it was also sung at her funeral. Her nickname was "Sunshine", too. Kelly's mom had a strong validation that her daughter was with her that day.

Still another time I kept hearing a piano playing soft music in my mind (Brahms, to be exact). I then went to a restaurant, before a reading, and there was a piano player playing the same music I was hearing from Spirit. I knew that it must be for an upcoming reading. Dan had a small piano recital for his family before he passed from cancer. During the reading, I explained to his mother that I heard Brahms, and she confirmed that it was his favorite music to listen to and to play on the piano. Dan wanted his mom to know that he connects with her during piano music so he encouraged her to listen and feel his presence.

Josh loved to play his guitar and shared his musical abilities with his brother in a band. When Josh's brother and parents came for a reading, I heard Josh playing some heavy rock on the guitar but did not recognize the tune. With his help, I understood the song to be "Blowin' in the Wind" by Bob Dylan. I conveyed the tune and they all cried. It was played at his funeral. So with clairaudience abilities, you might hear things in your head (or like me, right outside your head) or you might hear it literally coming from the real world (like your radio, a friend, someone who crosses your path, a movie, etc.). Be open and listen very carefully to all the methods that Your Child will creatively use to speak to you and sometimes through others and/or amazing "coincidences", which are truly gifts and not just random circumstances.

The most common way to communicate with Your Spirit Child is through the enhancement of your physical senses called clairsentience. Clairsentience involves obtaining messages through physical sensations, gut feelings, tastes, smells, or intuition. Feeling what is around you, and experiencing fleeting impressions that can affect your moods, and by doing so, you experience an emotional safety net catching your free-fall, and also connecting you with Your Child in Spirit.

It is far too easy to dismiss your own clairsentience abilities. I believe that the most healing aspect of any reading is that there is an enhanced sense of emotions and feelings from our Spirit Friends. The energy of Your Child is always around you, but in the presence of a good medium, the sensations you feel of Your Child will be amplified and enhanced, as if they are in the room with you. Many times, parents tell me that (regardless of the information that came through from Their Child in Spirit) most importantly they feel more connected and closer than ever before.

The vibration of Your Child will be intensified during a reading, which can result in the use of many facial tissues to wipe away the tears. Many times children give me the feeling of how they passed.

I could feel within my own body, for example, that Kelly had problems with her stomach and needed heavy medication (probably chemotherapy) to fight her cancer. She let me feel the pain that her body was undergoing before she passed and, more importantly, how the pain disappeared once she had crossed-over.

In connecting with Juan, he let me know of his fractured right femur and broken neck, from his accident, that caused his physical death.

Cheryl allowed me to feel the constant asthma and respiratory problems she experienced as a child. It is helpful that I have many years experience as an anatomist and that I understand the human body. This allows Your Child to give me specific information about his/her medical conditions for validation. I can feel the injury, disorder, or medical complications they experienced before passing.

Tim let his mom know (during a reading) how much his head hurt with dark thoughts about himself. He let me feel the confusion, the disappointments and the isolation he felt while here on earth. He wanted his mom to know that once he passed, he freed himself of the pain, and was sorry that she was feeling pain in her heart and stomach.

Children also allow me to feel if there is a physical or emotional problem with a family member. Monica came for a reading to find out how her son Bill was doing after passing from a motorcycle accident. Bill gave me the impression that his father was not feeling well, and that something was wrong in Dad's chest (I could actually feel it in my own body). Bill wanted his dad to seek medical help. Monica let me know that her husband needed bypass surgery and their Son in Spirit helped Dad get the assistance he needed before having a massive heart attack.

Karen came through to her parents to let them know that her little sister was very depressed, and needed attention for problems she was having with a friend, and how she was thinking of dropping out of college. Karen also let me feel how homesick her sister was, so that Mom and Dad could speak to her about the situation. Children in Spirit are our caretakers and very much want for us to feel peace, contentment, and joy in our lives here on Earth.

Being a medium is my greatest honor and accomplishment of this lifetime. To feel, hear, and see glimpses of the World of Spirit and convey the kind, compassionate and peaceful messages from Your Child in Spirit is the most healing experience I can encounter. It should be noted, though, that Your Child in Spirit gets the glory for creating the experience of connecting with you. I am simply the messenger, the 'phone instrument' to convey and transfer their love through me to you. I often laugh and tell my friends that growing up with my five sisters was good training for mediumship; I learned to be a good listener.

One of my favorite books is *The Little Prince* and in the book he says, "One sees clearly only with the heart. Anything essential is invisible to the eyes." Use your heart to communicate with Your Child in Spirit so that you can feel their vibrations and their whole new world of eternal existence that they wish to share with you.

Chapter 5
Through the Looking Glass

"Careful the things you say
Children will listen.
Careful the things you do.
Children will see.
Careful the wish you make
Wishes are children
Careful the path they take,
Wishes come true."

– *Lyrics By Stephen Sondheim, "Into the Woods"*

"Ready or not here I come!"

Your Child in Spirit is never hiding from you but your mind can hide the clues and signs they are showing or telling you.

A reading is a sacred and healing experience for you (as the sitter) receiving the energy and loving messages from the World of Spirit. The best way to prepare for a reading is to schedule one in advance so that no conflicts (except emergencies) can occur, and so that your Guides, and Your Child, can prepare to effectively communicate with you. It amazes me how many times a Child in Spirit will send a very special sign just before a reading, kind of setting the medium up and the Child saying, 'Did you see me?'.

Elaine came to hear from her daughter Rene who had passed several months prior to the reading. Rene kept placing pennies in her mom's path, almost every day of the week of the reading. When Rene told me to ask her mom if Mom collected the pennies, Elaine was elated.

She knew her daughter was with her and felt a sense of peace for the first time since her daughter's passing.

Andrew validated to his parents that he was near (prior to their reading) because they kept hearing his favorite saying, "Peace On". They overheard, several different times, complete strangers saying "Peace On" days before their reading.

You may want to write down some questions that are of concern to be asked during the reading. Know that there are no guarantees for specific answers to your questions. You may hear responses that are "180 degrees" from your prejudgment and logic. Remember that the "logistics" of a reading are very amazing. Think about this. A medium, living in the physical world, has to connect with the very subtle energies of Your Child at a very different level of vibration. Information may be passed on, from Spirit to Spirit, to a medium. The medium will then use relative associations based on personal experiences and, somehow, the "magic" in this process results in a beautiful healing message. For me, and many parents too, this is truly a miracle!

The medium has Spirit Guides working to help interpret the information being commu-

nicated and then must pass it on. Your Child
also has Spirit Guides working with them to
try to communicate information in a clear and
concise manner involving strong feelings. Talk
about "work by a committee"!

I remember reading for a very skeptical dad
one time, and his daughter acknowledged that
she knew that he was present at her bedside,
along with her little sister, just before her passing, and she acknowledged that Mom had left
her room for the first time in days. Dad said he
would believe that his daughter was communicating with him, if she would tell me what color
shirt he was wearing that day at the hospital. His
doubt blocked the beauty of his daughter's message of thanks for being with her before passing, and blocked the healing message, to Mom,
that it was alright that she was not present at her
daughter's passing. Mom already had the connection with her daughter, and it was Dad who
had to learn the lesson about the continuity of
life.

In preparation for a reading, you will find it
most helpful to be as calm and clear-headed as
possible (and even clear-hearted). It is under-
standable that you will be nervous in anticipation of hearing from your Loved Ones.

Your calm mind with help the medium connect with Your Spirit Friends and will help you listen more clearly to the information being presented. You may also wish to record the session in order to replay and rehear details of the reading at a later time. Many times, I have seen a parent become very nervous at a reading, they then get memory blocks, and are unable to confirm information or properly remember the information. I encourage parents to record the reading, or take notes, to review information presented, at a later time. Remember, Spirit is coming from a Higher Vibration of Wisdom and it is not fully expected that you will be able to confirm, or understand, all the information presented during the time of the reading.

Very frequently a parent will e-mail me days, weeks or months after their reading to validate information about some quiet little word, phrase, image or message that was communicated during the reading that, at a later time, they finally understood. Usually, Your Child in Spirit will communicate some type of message involving information that you do not know about. I find this very encouraging because Your Child is presenting information that exists which is separate from your mind; which means, I am not a 'mind reader', the information is truly coming from the Vibration of Spirit.

Stan told his mother, Estelle, from spirit that his father would go by the oak tree where his car crashed almost every day after work. Estelle was sure that this could not be validated information since her husband never mentioned this to her. Stan wanted his father to put his attention on the happy times they had camping, and fishing at the lake, and assembling model planes in the garage. Estelle contacted me, after the reading, to validate that it was true because her husband was visiting the crash site almost every day.

As with great moments filled with hopeful anticipation, it is best to come to a reading with limited expectations, and to be open, and allow the experience just to naturally unfold.

If you come to a reading with the anticipation of hearing from a specific person (like Your Child) then you can miss the "magic of possibilities" from the Other Spirit Guides who are present at your reading. Readings are like a Realtor's open house, in that all spirits are welcomed to come through. The fewer preconceptions you have, the happier you will be.

If Spirits feel a vibration in which they can express themselves with a message, they will come through. At times, a "friend-of-a-friend", or a relative of a friend, will have the need to come through your reading to pass on a loving or healing message. You should be open to accepting and receiving those messages from others, with love.

You, too, can be a messenger of The Light.

I remember reading for Stephanie. She was so focused on her son coming through, she missed all the beautiful messages her mom and her dad gave to her from Spirit. Stephanie's fear blocked her ability to communicate with her own parents and, in turn, to communicate effectively with her son. Her parents were trying to help Stephanie see how she could be more open to their healing presence and they provided some wisdom to help her to deal with her grief (but Stephanie was not open to listening). Also, in a beautiful way, her parents wanted to present her son to her; to let her know that he was in good hands, but Mom could not focus and acknowledge them, so the reading proved to be very challenging. Stephanie's own begrudging mind got in the way of her simply having a better experience during her reading. She missed an incredible Healing Message of Hope in which she could have found more happiness, trust, and faith-in-the-process of her life.

Usually, Your Spirit Guides know better than you what kind of information is going to be most helpful and healing. The more 'open' you are, to allow them to provide the necessary information for your reading, the clearer their messages. Your Child in Spirit has free will and they might not choose to come through during a specific reading. This does not mean they are not connected to you, it only means that Your Child in Spirit has things to do (to grow, develop, heal as a soul). Your Child in Spirit is still experiencing developmental growth of their soul, and may be busy working on a project at the time of the reading. They may have a project, event or situation that advances their development, healing, or evolution. And their attitude is, *Who are you to interrupt them?* Remember how often you might say, "Not now, Jimmy?" Well, "Jimmy" may now be busy, and may not want to hang out with Mom and Dad at that particular time. Your other Spirit Guides might want to provide some healing energy, and wisdom, to open you up, in order to more accurately hear from Your Child at a later time.

Accept and allow the light and love of Spirit to flow. It is also possible that a specific medium might not be able to connect with the energy of Your Child. 'Like energy' attracts 'like energy', so …if the Medium and Your Child have limited life experiences (such as feelings, symbols and signs) to share, then there might not be a good connection, although this is rare.

It is important for your incoming messages to be clear and specific, therefore, the medium (and their Spirit Guides) and those Guides of Your Child must have common ground in order to communicate effectively. For example, if Your Child wants to relate a message using symbols and signs related to football or baseball, and the medium has only experience with tennis and chess, then it may provide a more challenging opportunity for your son or daughter to communicate. Messages will get through but, again, if another relative in Spirit comes though, they might be able to communicate with greater efficiency about Your Child.

I recall communicating a message from Carla related to her experiences with the Girl Scouts but my limited knowledge about Girl Scouts made it more difficult for me to give better specifics about the badges she proudly earned. Carla's grandma came through and provided me with signs relative to Carla's gardening and cooking abilities, which helped her parents and me to realize her badges were related to those areas of her success in her Scouting days.

We all have Spirit Guides, and some of Your Guides walk with you throughout the physical life that you are now experiencing. Members of Your Spirit Group can change, though, as you have different experiences in your life. If you are challenged by a new job, or a new relationship, or you are experiencing obstacles in your path of life, an "expert" Spirit Guide may become a new part of your circle or team.

Steven decided to return to his hobby of refinishing furniture to help him heal through the loss of his son. Steven's grandfather, who worked for a varnish and paint furniture sales company while here in the physical plane, joined Steven's spiritual circle to provide grandfatherly energy in collaboration to refinishing furniture. If someone you loved passes (here on the earth plane) they, too, might join you as a Spirit Guide. It is almost certain that Your Child will join Your Spirit Circle and be of help to you from the other side. Imagine the magical beauty of Your Child giving clear-minded advice to you!

Usually relatives and friends (whether close or distant) are part of Your Spirit Team. Highly evolved souls, like Spiritual Masters and Angels, might also be part of Your Spirit Team to help you on the path of your soul's evolutionary ascendance.

Maude decided to study mediumship through books and spiritual circles so that she could become better familiar with her Spirit Guides and learn how to more easily communicate with them. She learned, in a reading, that Uthmia (a powerful enlightened healer from a South American Indian tribe) joined her circle to help her achieve her own spiritual enlightenment. You never know where help is going to come from but – good help is hard to find, and is always welcomed.

Your spiritual growth and development will be enhanced, thus fulfilling relationships with Your Spirit Guides, very similarly to how you develop meaningful relationships here in the physical plane with your friends and family. Get to know Your Guides and become familiar with their loving energy, communicate with them in 'prayer', and listen to their answers in 'meditation'. Connect to their vibration and be prepared to be inspired with their Wise Counsel and Healing Messages. Just learning who Your Guides are, during a reading, is worth the reading experience (so that you can work to build a strong relationship with them). Your life will be enriched and filled with more Hope and Compassionate Love just by knowing all the help you are consistently receiving from their healing energy.

There are several major modes used to communicate with Your Spirit Child. But, just as there are many different personalities of mediums, there are as many methods used by mediums to communicate with Spirit.

Use your intuition and choose a medium who is right for you. Some mediums like to use 'tools' to help them connect (tools like cards or crystals) while others like to hold objects that belonged to Your Child, to feel Your Child's vibrational energy. Some mediums may want to see a photograph or use Your Child's astrological chart to help guide them through a reading.

Remember, as discussed in the last chapter, the main type of mediumship that I have been sharing with you is referred to as 'mental mediumship' since it involves using the mind to connect with your Children in Spirit. Your Child in Spirit (and your other Spirit Guides, for that matter!) will give impressions in the medium's mind that will be communicated to you while receiving your reading.

It should be noted, too, that there are purely kinesthetic psychics and they have the ability to sense the information in your total body (i.e., the energy field or aura that exists around your physical body). As astonishing as it seems: not all psychics have the ability to communicate with Your Child in the World of Spirit. Psychics may be only sensitive to the energy you are giving off, and this is how psychics make readings based on your energy. A "medium" is an individual with psychic abilities who can communicate with the World of Spirit and, therefore, can connect with Your Child. So be sure to ask a psychic helper if he or she is a medium.

What is so beautiful and magical about a reading is that Your Child in Spirit, and your other Spirit Guides, will use very simple, but powerful and meaningful experiences, objects and words to share important memories that they carry with them (because they will always be part of their soul body). They know what knowledge is common to both the medium and the "sitter". For example, during one reading, Mickey Mouse was presented by a young girl named Claire. I know who Mickey Mouse is, but the meaning of Mickey Mouse to me meant a trip to Florida with my family when I was in the fourth grade. I presented the image of Mickey Mouse and the parents confirmed that Claire had a stuffed Mickey Mouse on her bed (a Mickey Mouse she received on a similar trip with her family).

Another example of commonality was the number 12 kept coming up from Mark, a young man who passed, to his mother. At first, Mom did not understand what he meant by '12', but there were many layers of meaning to his carefully chosen numeral. Mark's dad wore the number 12 when Dad played soccer as a youth (Mark also wore number 12 on his soccer jersey). It is the responsibility of the parent, receiving the reading, to fully embrace the many layers of meaning, and it usually takes some reflection time to "feel" the message's dimensions completely. Again, do not be disappointed if you do not remember information during the reading. Sometimes parents get 'psychic amnesia' when having a reading because they are nervous and excited. One time a mom forgot her son's first name, Franklyn, because he was always called by the name Thomas. After the reading, she corresponded with me and apologized for not validating her own son's actual birth name.

The sequence of Spirits who are presenting the context of the information, and the feelings experienced during the reading, are all powerful messages in their triplicate selves. With much reflection, after a reading, the wisdom of Your Child and Spirit Guides will become very apparent through the specific sequential language of communication that they specifically use.

The messages to a reading are like puzzle pieces putting themselves together. First, you create the border, and then you 'separate the pieces' by color. Once you begin fitting the pieces together, you create a very complete picture with many complimentary parts. Your reading will have many pieces and, once you fit them tighter, there too will be a very comprehensive message.

Often the puzzle's messages relate to very simple and precious moments shared with loved ones. Mary let her dad know how much she loved it when she and he sat on the porch swing and spoke about the evening stars. Timmy was eager to let his parents know how much he loved his new sneakers and all the places they visited when he wore them. Susan wanted to remind her parents about the many Christmas Eves when they watched a movie named *The Christmas Story* and ate dinner together. It is the simple moments, which carry incredible meaning, and that Your Child takes with him/her and holds eternally. Parents will often ask why Their Child shares these 'simple moments' when parents made *huge* efforts to do so many *costly* and *big* things together. I believe that a child in spirit, as others in spirit, appreciates the simple but loving moments in their lives. Whispers of kindness, compassionate exchanges, laughs, hugs and moments of caring are often expressed; not so much the momentous WHAT we did but the genuine HOW we shared our lives.

Often a child is *not* the first Spirit to come through during a reading for their parents. Other family members may come through initially, and I believe this is important because Mom and Dad then know that deceased relatives were there to meet their Child as a Son or Daughter entered into the World of Spirit. Relatives are usually very proud to present the Child to Mom and Dad and assure them that they are receiving loving care in Spirit.

Sally came for a reading and was so focused on hearing *only* from her daughter Jill that she was surprised how her mom and dad came first to share their messages with her. Sally was so happy to hear from Mom and Dad but, more importantly, she was elated to know that they had her Jill with them. Jill was relativity new to the World of Spirit and still had to orientate herself to the new way of communicating.

I encourage parents to give their Spirit Child at least several months to relate to his/her new surroundings, and to give them some time to adjust to heavenly life as well as giving parents adjustment time to accept a new earthly lifestyle. As when we are born here on Earth, we are challenged to become proficient in communicating. While Your Child is "born" into a New World of Spirit, it will take them some time to adjust to communication in a new telepathic way as well as giving parents adjustment time to accept a new earthly lifestyle.

It is also recommended that you limit the frequency of your reading to every three to six months. Your Child in Spirit will want you to progress with your own life and they have matters to take care of, too.

It is not beneficial for you to interfere with their progression (like picking at a scab when it's trying to heal). Also they do not want you to live day-to-day with information from readings. You have the ability to connect with Your Child in Spirit and they will always provide you with messages if and when you carefully listen or watch closely. Their messages are very rich with wisdom, and such words or feelings will give you much to think about, implement, and much motivation to improve in your life.

It is very important to give Your Child in Spirit the energy (and space) to grow and develop. The Taos Native American Indians customarily do not return to the cemetery to visit their departed loved ones after the funeral because they believe that in visiting the new grave, their visits keep souls or spirits here on the earth plane.

Think of Your Child's Soul on a kite string. If you give Your Child's Soul the length, to allow them to freely wander and explore, it is a magical journey. If you hold too tightly onto the "strings", they cannot discover and explore their new world.

Providing a reading for both parents can be very rewarding. Many times, one parent can help validate something that the other parent is unfamiliar with. For example, I was connecting with Joe (in spirit) and Joe was very concerned that his father was crying daily and needed professional counseling. Joe's mom said that this was not so, but Dad was present and admitted that he did need help with his sadness. Mom was amazed and Dad heard his son (from spirit) very clearly say to move on and give more attention to little John, Joe's younger brother.

Parents often ask if it is all right to bring siblings to a reading. There are a few important things to review. First, it is important for parents to be present when there is a reading for anyone under the age of sixteen. Children should also have a comprehensive understanding of mediumship and know what to expect during the reading. Remember that children are very open to Spirit Guides and sometimes it is helpful for living children to come to a reading to better understand the messages they are receiving and to discuss how they get those messages.

Marta and her mother had a "phone reading" to discuss Marta's little sister (Maya) who was coming through in dreams. Marta was open to receiving the messages from her sister, but it was important for Marta to understand that this was all right for her to have this ability (that her sister was still very connected to her, and that Marta had nothing to fear).

In-person and phone readings are equally effective in providing accurate messages because the Vibration and Energy of Spirit have no barriers. The best advice in choosing the type of reading depends more on how you best receive information. If you are a visual person, and want to feel a more one-on-one connection with the medium, then it is recommended that you sit with the medium in-person. Many times "Seeing is Believing" (although, I think, believing is seeing!). If you are a good listener, and feel more comfortable expressing your emotions over the phone (preferably at home) then this can be a better choice for you. A "phone reading" relies on great skill since there are no visual clues to the medium. You might feel disconnected on the phone, and prefer to experience the wonderful connection as only you can "in-person", though.

Readings are much more than validations from Your Child in Spirit that they are still conscious of your love and affections, although such awareness, in itself, can be very healing. Readings can provide you with very wise advice about how your soul can grow and develop in this lifetime.

It is common in most readings that you become aware of some basic Past Life Information to help you understand where you have been and where you are going. For example, Marcia came for a reading and her Spirit Guides told her that, in the last several lifetimes, she was unable to open her heart and love unconditionally. In a past life she had worked so hard, and isolated herself from the world, because she was afraid to love for fear of losing those whom she loved. The passing of her daughter was a very valuable Soul Lesson because, in this lifetime, she was experiencing a love for her daughter with no limitations or fears. She trusted the love she had for her daughter, and was told to take this message, and to understand that the trust she still holds for the love of her daughter will be eternal, no matter where her daughter is.

Messages can also provide helpful information about your overall physical health and emotional well-being. Often Your Child in Spirit, or Spirit Guides, will encourage a better diet, more exercise, meditation, reflection or a greater connecting with friends. The Spirit Messages can also provide information about how to help remove barriers in your family, and personal relationships, or career.

The most important attribute of any successful reading is for the parent to feel the presence of his/her child with greater intensity and love. The messages that come from Your Child, during a reading, are very important but the pure sensation of their energy is the most tender, hopeful and healing aspect of the experience. Countless times a parent has shared with me that they could finally relax and find more tranquility, after their readings, knowing Their Child was still connected with them and that Their Child's life is eternal.

It is essential for you to be very conscientious of the astonishing messages provided to you, and to listen with your heart. Reflect on the meaning in each message and understand that the signs and symbols provided have various layers of significance and value.

Don't frantically make information "fit" (out of desperation or fear) because it can lead to inaccurate messages and unsuitable implications. Allow your own subtle and guileless intuition to help you wisely determine the meaning and pure healing associated with the information you received.

Once you have the information, you are responsible to implement the ideas or changes that make sense to you. You have the insight, and power, to create the healing from the beautiful messages received from Your Child in Spirit. Children are listening, seeing and feeling from Spirit so be careful the things you think, say and do!

Chapter 6

Letting Go

"I'll be your candle on the water
My love for you will always burn.
I know you're lost and drifting
But the clouds are lifting.
Don't give up, you have somewhere to turn.

I'll be your candle on the water,
This flame inside of me will grow
Keep holding on, you'll make it,
Here's my hand, so take it.
Look for me, reaching out to show, as sure as rivers
flow,
I'll never let you go."

– Lyrics from Walt Disney's movie Pete's Dragon,
"Candle on the Water"

The passing of Your Child is one of the most emotional challenges you will ever encounter, which results in perhaps the most intense form of grief. It is important for you to understand that this loss can last the rest of your life. There is no way to quantify your grief, or to be truly empathetic, since no one else has experienced the exact situation. Grief is a personal journey and, although stages and steps can be associated with it, no one can identify your personal sorrow. The intention of this section of the book is to help you better understand what you are feeling and, more importantly, to let you know what Children from the World of Spirit feel about their parents who are grieving. Grief is like riding a roller coaster with its ups and downs, twists and turns, and an imbalance of such agonizing feelings.

The journey of grief involves many types of emotions from pain and suffering, anger and judgment, to guilt and regrets. Children in

Spirit, when they communicate during readings, often refer to these emotions and offer some wise and healing advice to their parents. One of the most consistent messages for parents (from their Children in Spirit) can be summarized nicely in one of Dr. Seuss' famous quotes, "Don't cry because it's over. Smile because it happened." Every moment of your life is a gift, be grateful and share the vibrations of gratitude and love.

The physical loss of Your Child can hurt you, but the greatest causes of your grief are your own thoughts. Your thoughts can take you to some dark places, with lower vibrations, that can cause great pain and suffering. A Teenager in Spirit referred to the repetitive thoughts, that her mother was constantly entertaining, like going through a House of Mirrors. Each time her mom reflected on her daughter's passing, the images became more distorted and unmanageably unreal.

Any endings in life can be uncomfortable, ("Life is a series of arrivals and departures"), but the passing of Your Child will be most uncomfortable. Sammy told his mom, in a reading, how he would get cold and she would always cover him up in a warm cozy blanket. He wanted his mom to wrap up her own cold thoughts and to start feeling comfortable.

The power of love, which you create and hold for Your Child in your heart, can help overcome the hurt. The higher Vibration of Love will dilute your pain and help you to heal. Miguel reminded his mother Regina, during a reading, that with every peanut butter and jelly sandwich she made for him it was filled with her tender affections. Although the sandwiches provided nutritional value to his physical body, Miguel wanted his mom to know that the most important sandwich ingredient was her compassion. Regina found comfort in knowing her son in Spirit could still acknowledge the love she shared with him. It did not completely heal her but it provided a buoyant life jacket in the Sea of Grief in which she had been drowning.

It may seem frightening that Your Child has gone, but they are just merely hidden from your physical senses. As in the game of Hide-and-Go-Seek, Your Child in Spirit wants you to find them! Their consciousness, their True Essence or Soul, is eternally present for you to discover, if you seek it. The eternal and formless consciousness Your Child's *is* cannot ever be lost because it is their true essence, forever. It is the part of Your Child that you will never lose. The consciousness of Your Child lives for all eternity and you have access to it, always. Keep in mind: Your Child reminds you, as presented in an earlier chapter, that they are much more than their physical body. The emotional, intellectual, and soul body of Your Child exists forever. They will share their emotions, thoughts, wisdom and desires with you if you are open to receiving them. Your intuition (or, that 'Knowing within you') will provide the clarity of truth that Your Child is eternal! You will find your true self as you seek the healing and blessings of Your Child's Higher Vibration.

Pain is the difference between what is and what you want it to be. Children remind parents often, in a reading, that pain is created by parents' very own egos. Your ego-mind wants to control your thoughts (like the controlling villain in a bedtime story). Your Child in Spirit always wants 'happily ever after' for you; so, honor them by conquering your 'dragon of fear'. Fears want to trap you into believing that: if you cannot have your way, then you will most surely suffer.

Pain consumes all aspects of your 'true self', it hurts you, it limits you, and it depletes energy from you. Pain reduces your creative abilities; it diminishes your capability to serve and connect with those whom you love (including Your Child in Spirit). It depletes your energy – it's like a deflated balloon with no propulsion to float toward Heaven. Pain limits your insight, your vision and, more importantly, it prevents you from obtaining your true nature: love. Pain and fear also weaken your physical body by draining your Energy Life Force which can result in disease.

Martha came to obtain a reading from me after the passing of her son (Jerry). She was a 45 year old woman who was living in a self-imposed 75 year old body. She had used all of her energy during the course of each day to focus on her self-imposed pain, and did not know how to live her life without grief and gloom. Her sorrow reduced her life to an isolated, dark and painful world. Jerry wanted so much for his mother to live, to breathe and open her heart to her family and friends whom she had abandoned in favor of seclusion and melancholia. He was concerned that she was not learning, on her Soul Journey, a valuable Lesson of Acceptance and Release. Jerry used the example of their canary, Tweedy, held within the confines of its cage.

Jerry would often open the cage door so that Tweedy could fly freely in the house! He wanted his mom to release her 'caged thoughts' and 'fly free' as well. Martha was more focused on what new diseases she was inviting and hosting in her body, almost as if they were guests visiting to honor her son. I only hoped that the "Tweedy" message from Jerry somehow changed Martha's way of thinking.

Many Children from Spirit are concerned for the pain their parents are enduring, and encourage parents to understand that their Children's non-physical aspects (souls) are with them forever and always.

I am not advocating that suffering is not necessary. For suffering can be a great and valuable teacher to us. It awakens our heart. Through suffering we better understand the depth of our compassion, and our love for any child, and for the beautiful love we have created.

Pain can also help a parent to be more sensitive, caring and compassionate to others.

Suffering is necessary, until it no longer serves us, and then we can become more ready to heal. Suffering disappears when you bring your thoughts to the present moment and accept your life (and the life of Your Child) just as it is, with no more judgments. Remember, your view of their passing is humanly limited and their perfect passing is in line with the Universal Clock.

Your Child in Spirit does not want you to live in the past. "Be with me now, accept me as I am now", Your Child in Spirit often tells me during a reading. They also caution you to not live uncontrollably into the future, either! Sometimes a grief stricken parent will say, "I wish it was 'my time to go' so I may be with my Child in Spirit". They wish away the beautiful gift of their own life as if it does not matter or that it has no value or meaning. Living in the Now will bring you peace and joy because: pain and suffering cannot exist without the imposition of the past or the worry of the future. Remember that when Your Child leaves the physical world, to go on a trip to the World of Spirit, it is not 'good-bye', rather it is, "See you again!". You connected with them once, you can connect with them again (and again). You can best feel their presence when you focus on, and stay in the now. Find them in the Vibration of Love within your own heart and keep them there!

Children often tell their mom and dad that it is the parents' own thoughts that cause parents unnecessary pain. Simply put, "Pain is self-imposed if you do not get things the way you want them!" Pain comes from within the ego, arrogantly insisting that you know what is best, and where and how to find what it is you want (in children we call that being 'spoiled' or "The Terrible Two's"). "Pain is inevitable; suffering is voluntary."

Many times parents believe that they know what is best for the Soul of their Child! Pain that dominates most parents is the desire and want of their child to remain with them in the physical plane, even if their child has completed their life lessons, has a physical body that can no longer properly function, or if the soul does not have the desire to remain in the physical body ("Can we say the words: 'Parental Tantrum'?").

Tony came through to his father, in a reading, and gave his father the message that his body could no longer sustain Tony's soul. Tony held on for many days longer than even doctors thought possible from the brain injuries of an automobile accident. Tony wanted to give his dad time to come to terms with Tony's ultimate passing. Dad could not let go, but Tony could no longer spiritually stay in a dying body with an injured brain. Dad was so hurt that Tony left, but it was Tony's will to leave 'a shell' that no longer could serve his soul.

Free will is the natural state of being; the gift from God. Allow Your Child's free will to 'cross over' peacefully, into the tranquility and serenity of the World of Spirit. They can only cross over into Spirit if it is the will of God, anyway.

Truthfully, a parent can know how to best help their child find their way in the physical plane. Ultimately though, it is best to allow our children to find their way in life through their own personal experiences.

We cannot truly know someone unless we have drunk from their 'sippee' cup, felt their experiences, shared their beliefs and become intimately familiar with their thoughts.

Your view is limited by your own experiences, beliefs, fears and attitudes and even your perception of your own child's physical life. To love them does not mean that you know them. Imagine how limited you are in trying to understand Your Child's Soul, when a soul is so complex with only one soul's many lifetimes.

How many previous lifetimes has Your Child experienced, and how has each lifetime affected and molded whom they are? What value and what wisdom does this lifetime (brief as it may have been) create for Your Child's Soul that they can put in the 'treasure chest' of their causal body? Children from Spirit remind parents, many times, that the parents' limited and personalized view cannot fully comprehend and understand the vastness and unlimited potential of a child's soul (or your own soul, for that matter).

With love and trust you must believe and hope that the Universe has provided the best possible outcome for Your Child.

Annie and Clair, twins of just 16 weeks, passed from complications in their underdeveloped respiratory systems. They came and left the physical plane together as two peas in a pod. The twins communicated (in a reading to their parents) that they were extremely grateful for their gift of life and the selfless decision that their parents made to allow the twins to cross over into Spirit. Annie and Clair wanted their parents to know that they could have lived for a long time with machines attached but, as Highly Evolved Spirits, they only needed to be here for a brief period in order to review a lesson learned in a previous life. Through the event of their tiny physical bodies' swift passing, they also wanted to awaken their parents to the continuity of life and the greatness of love from the World of Spirit. Their parents' outlook about their lives has changed significantly since the passing of their twins because of the messages that were being provided to them. Annie and Clair explained that they have a much greater appreciation for the precious gift that each day of life offers and that they now spend more time on the things that really matter, like the relationship they have with their son and their parents.

Nothing external to your mind can hurt you unless you give it the power to do so. No one but yourself affects you.

Your thoughts can establish your mood, attitude and affect your beliefs. Stuff happens to all of us. The difference is how you think of it and respond to it. Does it become your servant or your tyrant? Your stepping stone or your stumbling block? Through the passing of Your Child, do you cherish and appreciate the gift of having had them with you, each bright smile, and each comforting hug to warm your heart? Or do you allow your pouting ego to bury you in pain and would you rather focus on what you do not have? You demonstrate to the Universe who you are by how you respond. And your response then draws into your life the Energy associated with it. Remember teaching your infant to walk? When Your Child fell, with their first wobbly steps, you encouraged them to get up and keep walking. They encourage you to pick yourself up and start 'walking' through life again! Or would you rather pout, sit and whine? And: What good does that do?

Mary was an amazing mother and strong soul. Her son acknowledged in a reading his great appreciation, and handed his mother thousands of pink roses (her favorite kind)! When her teen-aged son passed because someone else's son had too many birthday drinks, crossed the double line, and hit her son head-on, Mary directed a loving response by establishing a local chapter of MADD (Mothers Against Drunk Driving) and worked with teenagers at the local high schools to encourage no drinking, especially when driving. His death was celebrated with support, care, and compassion to help others who might make similar choices that could end lives. Who knows how many children Mary helped to take the right action and prevented the loss of other teenagers? It is beautiful to me to witness a parent in pain honoring and respecting their child with healing acts of kindness despite their own personal sense of loss.

In another reading, Estelle came through to her mom with paint brushes. Estelle's mom was an artist and established a Grief Camp for other despondent mothers. She helped other moms deal with the passing of their children through the creative and emotional expression of painting, drawing, and creating clay pots.

Darren and Lucy were the proud parents of Danny. When Danny was twelve years old, he passed from leukemia. Before passing he helped many of the younger children in the cancer ward feel better with the use of video games, and stories of princesses, knights and dragons. Danny came through to his parents and acknowledged how proud he was that they developed a leukemia foundation in his honor. His parents raised money for families who were having financial difficulties for the costly treatments. Darren and Lucy raised thousands of dollars and honored their son like a knight (through their specific act of kindness, and by slaying the ego mind dragon of hopelessness).

The pain of grieving is a sign that you do not understand 'who you are' and the power you possess. Grieving comes from the belief that you are powerless. You have potential just like Your Child's battery-operated, laughing "Susie Doll".

If you laugh, when you laugh, you can recharge your battery and find peace. 'I can't', 'I am unable', 'I am lost' are all voices of the ego that Children in Spirit want you to stop saying!

Tina wanted her mom to replace her constant worried vocabulary of 'I can't' with the words of one of her favorite childhood books, *The Little Engine That Could*. "I think I can, I think I can", said the train as Tina relayed the message to me during the reading.

Pain is a villain that finds its pleasure in making parents give into their egos and thus weakening the bound of love. You are less likely to experience the beautiful connection of Your Child in Spirit if you block your love for them with pain. Children in Spirit often remind parents that pain is a barrier; it causes them to vibrate at a lower frequency, inhibiting parents' ability to connect with their child who is now at a Higher Vibration in Spirit. Your Child is always present on this plane when they cross-over, but it is only your state of mind, your energy that will allow you to hear, feel and experience their presence. Like forms of energy attract like forms (so if you vibrate at a higher frequency through love, compassion and joy you are more likely to connect Your Child in Spirit).

Often I have parents come to a reading frustrated because they cannot feel the presence of their Child in Spirit or they cannot dream about their Child. Again, if the parent is saturated with pain and suffering, then they are existing at a lower frequency, a lower vibration while their Child is at a higher vibration. Keep in mind that Your Child is always present, but if your state of mind is vibrating with lower frequency thoughts, then you can be blocked or inhibited from hearing, seeing or feeling Your Child's presence. Radio waves exist at all different frequencies in "the field," and if our sound systems aren't tuned in to a specific frequency you cannot hear or receive the incoming message.

No one should ever tell you to ignore the feelings you possess, especially with the loss of a child. What is important, though, is to not allow your life to become lost. Your Child would not want that for you and you should not want that either. In almost every fairy tale you read to them, the tales remind you that it's about finding what you lost, conquering fear, and coming home to love.

Besides your own children, you always have others to serve through your life's work. Focus on the loving experiences you had with Your Child and experiences you can still have. When it is their birthday, celebrate with a cake and acknowledge their presence. Children in Spirit often encourage Mom and Dad to talk to them, they are listening. Focus your thoughts and energy on today, as much as possible, because you will find the peace and serenity of Your Child's Energy in this moment! Do not get lost in the past. Pain is exposed when we go back and relive painful memories, over and over again, instead of focusing on the new relationship you are establishing with Your Child.

Christy's son, George, passed fourteen years ago when she came for her reading. She was frustrated and confused why God would allow her to still have such pain over George's death. She relived his car accident and continuously thought about it, spoke about it (ad nauseum) and tenaciously would not let it go. For fourteen years she developed a wall around herself because her family and friends could not help her remove this pain and they did not want to keep experiencing it themselves. Christy thought that if she let go of the pain, then she was letting go of the connection to her son. George made it clear, in the reading, that his mom was holding him on a short 'kite string'. He was unable to grow as a soul because her pain was keeping him close (and he feared for her safety!). He asked her, each day, to let out 'a little more string' so he could fly and so that she could be more open to his presence. One year later, Christy contacted me and let me know that much of the pain was gone, she was now having vivid dreams of her son, and she knew he was speaking to her through music and a new symbolic language. In letting go of the pain, she opened herself up to a new type of relationship with her son! A healthier, happier relationship for her, for him, and all of her friends and family whom she had previously been alienating!

No one wants to consciously be in pain. It is our subconscious mind that sometimes holds the 'remote control' of how we feel. Good news: You can overcome pain by acting like a child again! Our Children are great examples of how we should experience day-to-day life. Laugh, sing, dance, color, just play and play hard.

Joey told his dad, in a reading, that the more Dad played: the closer Joey would feel a connection with Dad. They used to love to play tennis together, and Dad was avoiding tennis because of the memories he had of playing with Joey.

But when Dad began to play tennis again, Dad's pain lightened up and he actually felt his son's presence at the game.

Connect with your friends when in pain. Do not focus on the pain but focus on the joy of sharing energy! Children in Spirit have advised their parents to go on trips, and explore new locations, situations, and experiences. As with the outline of every bedtime story and dream you share, continue on your journey, seek new beginnings and new horizons and celebrate a new life. Enjoy the wisdom of nature; increase your vibration with a new hobby (draw, paint or color). Think like a kid, and you will begin increasing your vibration and you'll start being happier and happier. Blow bubbles!

Our children can be great teachers, especially when it comes to dealing with anger. Aside from the 'Terrible Twos', when someone occasionally takes a toy away from Your Child, they can be mad for a few moments but usually their "rage" passes, and then children are onto another toy.

When a child is "taken" from their parents, the adults have a hard time getting over the anger! Anger is not your true nature. When you display anger, you are acting from fear. Through anger you are attempting to make someone else feel as badly as you do (recall George's mom Christy and how badly she made family and friends feel).

Usually when we think that we are inadequate, incomplete, or we lack something: we attack those we love. When you attack, you only feel the pain and hurt within yourself. We attack what we fear, and this only makes us more vulnerable, gives us more suffering and immerses us in more pain. The greater the anger, the more frequent the attacks, which cause separation, isolation and despair.

Joe was so angry when his only son (Joe, Jr.) passed that he could not control it. For years he made harsh judgments against Hispanics because his son was accidently hit by Jose. Joe, Sr. lost many friends, and his wife of ten years, because his irrational racist anger uncontrollably overcame him. During his reading, his son encouraged his father to let go and that, in attacking others, he was really asking for help. Joe, Jr. so wisely communicated to his dad that his dad was only attacking others because he was subconsciously asking for help, support and was in great need of healing!

When you carry love in your heart, you retreat from attacks, and you soften the anger. "It is much harder to judge yourself than to judge others. If you succeed in judging yourself, it's because you are truly a wise man," *The Little Prince* reminds us.

The major suffering from the loss of Your Child is your judgment of their death as being a "bad" thing, a horrible occurrence! Once you *name* things, you judge them and, in judging things, you separate yourself from the source of all good: God.

Nothing that happens is an isolated event. Everything and everybody is interconnected. When we isolate specific incidents and label them as "bad", we judge them without a comprehensive knowing. In the Master Plan of the cosmos (or God's Plan) the passing of Your Child is just as it is supposed to be. Their passing may be an opportunity for another Child's Soul. For example, if Your Child passes from the results of an alcohol related car accident, it is an opportunity for other children's consciences to make better choices. Your Child's passing might be a growth opportunity for your soul. Perhaps your soul is seeking to trust that love, and life, is eternal and that what cannot be seen is still very real. You are allowed to face your own mortality and have the conscious choice of healing. Their passing might be an opportunity for the growth of their own soul.

Possibly Your Child had completed its soul lessons in this physical lifetime and is now ready to progress forward. It is impossible for you to know the reasons why, but the 'why' is energy draining. Replace your whys with gratitude, and with reassurances that someday Your Soul's Energy and Your Child's Soul Energy will be reunited! Replace whys with faith, and new found rivers of joyful causes and living!

It is the distressing call from your ego to harm, snarl and worry. Do you honor yourself (and Your Child) through fear? For every illness, accident, or disaster, there is the potential for salvation and liberation elements that we are probably not even aware of. Many times Your Child from Spirit will help you bring your focus to the world of the unseen, the World of Spirit. They will tell you that their physical form is an illusion and that their passing is just as natural as their birth. It is a sacred privilege to be present at their passing. Just as you were with them, birthing them into the physical world, so shall you be with them as they peacefully 'birth' into the World of Spirit.

The love you have for Your Child cannot coexist with guilt. If you allow your ego-mind to fill you with guilt, then you are denying the love you have for yourself and Your Child. Your own condemnation injures and hurts you. Do you believe that this is what Your Child in Spirit would want for you? Guilt wants you to punish yourself, it wants you to suffer and feel pain. Is this honoring yourself? Is this honoring Your Child in Spirit? Spirit's quick answer is: "No".

Children in Spirit often communicate with great compassion and a strong will that they do not want their parents to disrespect themselves with guilt, which blocks their Child's heart from providing the energy of love to the parents.

Desiree wanted her father to find *peace again in his life,* but he was harboring so much guilt because he did not drive her to school the day that she was hit by a car. She reminded her father that he was going to work early that day so he could (with all good intentions) make it to her art show that afternoon. His proactive plans, on the day she passed, were tainted with a 'guilt trip' of how he hadn't driven her to school. Desiree also reminded her father that it was her time to pass and that she was so at peace with her kitty, Felix, that had also passed and that she was still creating beautiful art in heaven.

In accepting guilt for yourself, you are blaming yourself for something—or feeling you have done something wrong. You are admitting remorse for having done something out-of-sync. Have you sinned? Did Desiree's father 'sin' for the intention of going to work early so that he could attend her art show that day? We are much harder on ourselves than any child, who has passed, would ever lovingly want us to be.

Such useless guilt is feeling responsible for circumstances that were not ever in your control. Many times, when a child decides to commit suicide, the parents express overwhelming guilt. Susan had her adult son move in with her because his severe drinking problem did not allow him to make healthy choices for himself. She helped him through rehabilitation twice, provided a car for him, gave him food and love. Tom eventually took his life, and all Susan could do was to blame herself. She could conjure up hundreds of reasons why it was her fault. She did not, however, provide: the gun, the thoughts, or even the fear for Tom to make his choice to end his life. She did everything that a loving parent would do. Tom wanted her to know that she was not responsible for his choice, and that her love had prevented him from leaving sooner than he intended because of her immeasurable caring. During the reading he did not want his pain, his fears and his suffering to influence his mother. This was his choice, and his choice only, and he let his mother know that she could not have done anything to change the outcome. Whew! What a relief! But only if we wish to be relieved.

The most overwhelming guilt I have encountered during readings though, is the feeling of loss and shame for not having done or said something to someone who has passed over.

Mary felt guilty because she thought her daughter's boyfriend was not to be trusted. He ended up killing her daughter, Sandy, but she accepted the responsibility for Sandy's death. Over and over, again and again, Mary blamed herself for Sandy's passing (as if she had the knife in her own hands). Sandy communicated during the reading that Mary must forgive herself so that Mary might find peace and well-being in her life again. Sandy reminded Mary how many heated disagreements about Sandy's boyfriend occurred, and how many times Mary warned Sandy that she had a bad feeling about Sandy's boyfriend. As a soul, Sandy wanted her mother to know that she had taken responsibility for her own actions, and that her boyfriend could not destroy her soul or the love she had received from her mother. "Mom needs to let go of the guilt so that her heart can love again," Sandy communicated.

The most energy draining word that I hear from parents is "regret". It is their Children from Spirit that remind their parents that, at any given moment, parents can make a choice; the best possible choice *for that moment.*

Your choice will affect your soul and the souls of many others; your choices become layers of wisdom traveling in all dimensions with you as the wellspring. Your choice then journeys outward, in waves of energy, like ripples across the calm pond after dropping a rock into it. Ten minutes, ten hours, ten months or ten years from now you can reflect on your choice and reconsider it. Your energy also crashes like waves on the rocky coastline, onto the contentment of the now, and can drown you with the sorrow of the past (washing over your center of peace and saturating you with the most energy draining question of all: why?). What value will second-guessing have to you and to those you love by giving energy to something that cannot be changed – the past? The best question is, "What Good Thing can come from this?".

Regrets are unrealistic expectations from your ego to be someone that you are not, to do something that you did not do, or to question an action that you performed. You did the best you could do at a given moment in time. Even though now you may have a different vantage point, looking back at a situation, it doesn't mean you didn't do your best.

Angela was pleased to connect with her daughter (Stacy) in a reading. Stacy passed six months earlier, in a drowning accident, at a local lake where she was swimming by herself. Regret after regret filled Angela's mind of as to "*Why did I let her go, why didn't I tell her for the twentieth time not to swim alone, why didn't I go with her, why didn't her father tell her not to swim alone, why did her friend Trudy leave her by herself, why, why...why?*" Angela saturated herself with so much regret it took the loving and kind words of her Child in Spirit to make her aware of her regrets so that Mom would begin to heal.

Your scope of vision is much greater on Today's Peak of a Mountain than from Yesterday's Hidden Valleys below. The energy used to try to rewrite your past history is meaningless (and filled with the ego's self-pity!). Yes, maybe you could have had the talk before 'he left for work and had the accident', or maybe you could have recommended 'counseling for the fourth time before she took her own life'. Your Child's choices are not your responsibility, and they want you to know this with some conviction from their wise vantage point in spirit.

You are only responsible for your own choices and your responsibility is based on the information, beliefs, knowledge and wisdom you have at that specific moment.

Fred was the star quarterback for his winning high school football team his senior year. His parents knew that he had a slight heart murmur of several years but his health appeared exceptional. On a hot autumn day, Fred was sacked and never awoke. An autopsy revealed that Fred had a dysfunctional heart valve that broke just before his passing. His parents and doctors did not know of the problem valve and therefore should not feel regret (so their son made sure he communicated that idea during a reading). The information that Fred's parents had about his good health before his passing, is the fact of the matter (and if his parents had any idea that he had a defective heart valve they could have provided different recommendations to their son's activities). "No regrets, please," Fred communicated through me, "Remember to be 'defensive' against your ego-mind thoughts!"

As you look back now you might think differently but, does that not confirm that you grew from the experience? You were offered a valuable opportunity to learn something because you see it differently now. But this is now, and that was then. Regrets are useless energy that will impede your development as a soul. Would you shred good money in a paper shredder? Your life is "really abundant and valuable cash," and regret does nothing but "shred you up!"

Imagine if you accept that you were *supposed to be doing* just as you did and nothing more nor less; that you were to be *exactly who you were* and no one else! Alice was baking cupcakes for her daughter Darlene's twenty-second birthday. Darlene was away at college, and riding her bike back to her dorm, when a car struck her and she passed. Darlene reminded her mom Alice (in a reading) that her mom was in the act of icing the cupcakes when she passed, as a way to express that her mom always was "the icing" on her life. Alice felt regret for not being with her daughter, when she passed, but her Darlene reminded her that it was Mom working extra hours (to help pay for college) and Mom who drove her to all those soccer practices resulting in Darlene's soccer scholarship. In so many ways, Mom made Darlene's life so much richer and sweeter. "No regrets, only gifts," Darlene told her Mom!

Acceptance is the power of living in the present moment with respect for self, responsibility for all involved in any given situation (even your Spirit Guides!), and trust of Universal Proportion and Providence. Regrets require you to focus on the past, but the 'past' does not exist today except in your ego mind. The past is history, and history is but a record to compare your standards, and to grow, and a starting point from which to expand your consciousness. The past cannot be changed but YOU can change the way you *think* about the past. The past takes away the immediate moment's energy to create in the present moment.

There are several types of regrets that I experience frequently as a medium doing readings for "ashamed" parents. First, there are the regrets for not doing something a certain way; doubting that a specific action, formulated even out of unconditional love and executed with good intentions, was somehow not right! As if you should have had the insight, foresight, or precognition to know that you could have done things differently!

Well, sure: you could have done things differently if you knew beforehand the results of every action someone else is creating. And how many people are there on the planet? Usually we can take some type of action, but soon we question that action, repeatedly, and think we should have done more.

For example, suppose that you notice that your son is really tired, and you encourage him to 'stay home from work today'. Your son goes to work, falls asleep at the wheel of his car and has an accident. Now: was it your fault that he did not listen to your caring recommendation? Did you create the action of the accident, or were there other factors, or forces involved? If you always spent all of your day second-guessing every decision you made then you would miss the opportunities to create in the present moment.

A second type of regret is the guilt for doing nothing!

You can burden yourself with the responsibility of not doing anything to try to prevent someone else's activity. The truth is that the action would not have happened if it were not supposed to. How can you expect to know the consequences of every action when every action has a multiplicity of layers of interaction and results? You can only see the world through your limited scope of vision and so maybe your choice was to help someone else, which leads to huge implications of helping many others.

I always like to think of the movie *It's A Wonderful Life* when Jimmy Stewart gets the opportunity to see how his noble actions helped so many people, on so many levels, throughout his life. Live a noble life! We do not create the actions of others. The lack of action just means you are not focusing on the action you were supposed to be concentrating on but, rather, always act nobly as your calling! We cannot take responsibility for someone else's choices; we are only responsible for our own dignified behavior. If we did not take an action, then it was the will of others to create a specific result. It is not reasonable to think you can control someone's freewill, and to think so is the penultimate arrogance!

A third type of regret is doing something that you do not want to in order to try and please others. Do you believe if someone really loves you they would want you to do something that you do not want to do? Love is supposed to be fully realized when it has no limits and no conditions. Here we get to the questions of intent. Regrets are based many times on living our lives based on the decisions of others. Who controls your thoughts – Mom, Dad, your Pastor, your Boss – or are you in charge?

The world cannot possibly know how you should be. You are perfect as you are. To change in order to fulfill someone else's desire (getting a college degree, or accomplishing a specific task) must be from your own desires and incentive if you want to best serve others and find peace of mind. In changing your desires because of outward, meddling influences, you compromise your beliefs, attitudes, abilities and most importantly, your service to others. It is only through knowing what you are "most passionate about" that you can achieve optimal service to others and find peace of mind.

Your Children in Spirit tell me, always, how regrets are an appalling waste of energy! You cannot build on regrets, you cannot grow from your regrets, and all you can do is bury yourself deep in the annoyances, aggravations and frustrations of the past. We must discard permanently the burden that we are imposing on ourselves with all of this useless regretting. Forgive ourselves, and accept and allow the present moment to fill our minds with peace and joy! How will you know if you don't at least try? Remember how you always encouraged Your Child to try strawberry instead of always vanilla, to dream about butterflies instead of caterpillars, to conquer the monster under the bed, to discover the stars and to sing praise and not cry fear? Walk the talk. Walk in light!

Rediscover your life and stop demanding that your Child in Spirit be that life; move forward, just as they have moved on, as they want you to do. Do not "run the race" by always looking over your shoulder. Nobody wins a race by looking where they *have been*, but rather, by keeping their eyes on the prize.

Kids are the best examples of living in the moment. Live in the precious present, Mom and Dad! Your Kids in Spirit are "your candles on the water." Remove yourself from the black river of grief. They offer you their little hands, to guide and reassure you, so take them. Hold on to the hope, embrace the love, and welcome the peace they 'gift' to you. They'll never let go!

Chapter 7

Over the Rainbow to Divine Love

"You'll be in my heart
I'll be there from this day on,
Now and forever more.
You'll be in my heart
No matter what they say
I'll be with you
You'll be in my heart
I'll be there
Always."

– Lyrics from Walt Disney's movie Tarzan,
"You'll Be in My Heart"

Your Son or Daughter is a loving gift of God; a precious present that is eternally yours. Your Child is an expression of God, a piece of God's eternal presence, an everlasting beam of God's enlightenment. Every moment you share with Your Child is a treasure. You get the opportunity to contribute your affection, care, kindness, and wisdom with the soul of Your Child with every laugh, every smile, every coloring book page colored, every cookie shared, and every game you ever played.

In Chapter One of this book, I spoke of a wise child with a golden smile named Elizabeth, who I had the fortunate experience of playing several board games with and learning precious lessons (about the natural processes of life and death and the continuity of life). These memories will be with me for evermore and the wisdom that Elizabeth shared with me will be everlasting. What memories do you have with Your Child in Spirit?

The nice thing about love is that you can always freely give it. Children in Spirit know this, and often express to their parents the following: love from the heart and not the head.

Love from the head is love that is used to gain, to control, or regulate the emotions, feelings, beliefs or actions of another individual. It really is not love, but rather it is the use of affections and fear, together, to control an outcome. Examples are, "Sally, I will give you a new dress if you clean your room." "Jimmy, I will increase your allowance if you improve your grades in school." Can you see the conditions associated with the giving in these rewards? If love is not given freely, then it is certainly not the love of God or what my Spirit Guides refer to as Divine Love.

Love from the heart is known as Divine Love (or some call it unconditional love) and this is love that is of God. Man does not have to be in Spirit to receive Divine Love (we can receive Divine Love in the flesh!). The soul of everyone is capable of accepting and expressing Divine Love.

Love is abundant and plentiful. There are no limits, no boundaries to giving love. Children remind me in spirit to celebrate Christmas, Hanukkah and birthdays. Remember, in giving a present, we receive the pleasure, the satisfaction, and the love of sharing. In giving love, you show love for self and allow it to come to you and through you. Children in Spirit often remind their parents, in a reading, that in giving the gift of love, you actually are giving to yourself. Since we are all 'one', by loving others, we love ourselves.

God is love! Divine Love is the awareness of your soul as part of God; therefore, it is the awareness that "you also are love". If you express your consciousness with the innocence of a child, you will find your way back home: Heaven. You will connect with Your Child in an uncomplicated and trusting way when you lovingly speak their language of innocence.

The truth of the matter is, that your soul is the center of the purest form of love: Divine Love. Divine Love is love with no restrictions, no stipulations or attachments, and is the only language of the World of Spirit. To master this love you must be able to share, give, and contribute love with no expectations in return.

The love you have for Your Child in Spirit will require you to accept two integrative aspects of love: trust and faith. Divine Love does not exist without the conviction of faith and the confidence of trust.

With the transformation of Your Child into Spirit, you are asked to have Faith in the love you have for Your Child. Edgar Cayce said, "Faith is a bridge that spans the gulf from the seen to the unseen." Faith means that you are willing to accept the eternal love, from and to, Your Child in Spirit, without any basis of reason, beyond what your physical senses can perceive and by having no doubts. It is your duty to accept faith, develop your faith, use your faith and enjoy the rewards you create in your life through faith. Faith is of Spirit, it is of God. Do not let the trials of losing Your Child allow you to sink into depression and perish with hopelessness. It is your responsibility to view all aspects of life from a spiritual perspective and accept them in a spiritual way.

Use your faith and it will strengthen you. No one can teach you faith, and no one can destroy your faith. You can enlighten others through the use of faith, and you can be the light and hold steadfastly to the gift that is given to you from God. Have faith in Divine Love that you and Your Child in Spirit can share, experience and express love eternally.

Every situation is an opportunity to grow, to love, and to learn. The passing of Your Child is a precious chance for you to love from a new perspective. You get the opportunity to experience love in a new way, in a way that challenges your beliefs, that challenges the truth, and to express love in a most trusting way. Is complete love, ever possible, without full trust?

To trust in love is to believe in love with all your heart. With loving Your Child unconditionally comes your responsibility to accept and allow the choices that they choose to make both in their physical and spiritual realms. If Your Child made a spiritual pact with you (to leave early) then you, too, must honor this agreement by allowing them to freely fly heavenward! In accepting their departure from the physical plane you are supporting their spiritual evolution and your own. In accepting, you allow for them to fly from your arms into the embrace of God. For, in the arms of God, Your Child unites with the sacred, tender and compassionate vibration of their creator, your creator. Would you want anything less for Your Child when you are expressing unconditional love for them? Remember, because you and Your Child are from the same sea of energy, there is never any separation. The energy of love vibrates at the highest frequency possible, for those who are separated from us, and re-unites us with Heaven.

God dwells within you in the form of grace. Grace is the acceptance of the Divine Love that God has for you. Grace is within you and all others. If you trust, then you have love because it is impossible to have love without trust. It is easiest for you to realize the grace God has for you with a quiet mind; a mind stilled and calmed by peace.

Your Child chose you, from the World of Spirit to be their parent. You helped manifest the situations and circumstances that were necessary for Your Child's soul to grow and develop in their most recent lifetime. Your contributions, to their physical experience, were part of their karmic growth (and yours, too!) that they will utilize to cultivate and expand their soul.

Your ego challenges you to continue accepting the grand illusion but, if Your Child is no longer wearing his/her physical body, then they are simply separated from you but NOT cut off from you! There is no force, no circumstance, and no obstacle that can ever truly separate you from Your Child. How can you separate Your Child and yourself, both aspects of God, if only by the conviction of the ego within your mind? The shortest distance between where you are and where you ought to be is: inside your head—your mind. Change your thoughts and you can change your life!

Imagine the joy you can create in your life when you change your mind to thoughts of forgiveness; especially forgiveness for self. The greatest triumph of your soul is to forgive. To forgive is to find the blissful tranquility of heaven. By forgiving, you raise your vibration to its greatest potential frequency in the physical plane and you thereby travel over the rainbow. *"Somewhere over the rainbow, Way up high, There's a land that I heard of once in a lullaby. If happy little blue birds fly, Beyond the rainbow, Why oh why can't I,"* sang Dorothy in the Wizard of OZ.

Forgiveness offers all that you seek; peace, happiness, stillness, and beauty.

It is easy to excuse Your Child if they eat too many cookies, don't clean their room, stay out past their curfew or get a speeding ticket. A true tribulation of your soul comes when you are offered the opportunity to forgive someone, or something, who was involved in the passing of Your Child. To forgive a bacterium, the rain or wind, a drug, a tumor, a gene, or a fearful thought, can all be your soul's means of acquiring great wisdom and the peace of God.

Children in Spirit regularly communicate to me that it is essential for their parents to first and foremost forgive themselves in order to heal from their child's passing. Forgiveness is the 'ABCs' of the language of unconditional love, the only language that Your Child in Spirit speaks. It is the means for a parent to connect with Your Child and continue a relationship. As the ad says, "Don't leave home without it!" Don't continue Life without Forgiveness.

Your Child in Spirit communicates to me, during readings, with a consistent theme: 'It is easier to forgive when you live in the present moment.' Forgive the past and let it go because it is already gone. It is important to Your Child in Spirit for you to live in this very moment, the present moment. It is in the present moment that you understand, and connect with your true nature and their abiding, regenerating presence. It is in this moment, the now, that you have the free will to think, feel and believe what you choose. Accept Divine Love in this moment, surrender to Divine Love, and find freedom in Divine Love in this moment.

Fear is not of the present, but only of the past and future, which do not exist in the present. Only the past can separate you from Your Child in Spirit. The regrets of yesterdays separate you from Your Child in Spirit; the worries of tomorrows separate you from Your Child in Spirit. Heaven is here; heaven is in the now! Choose to reside in the House of the Here and Now.

Forgiveness is the answer to happiness; it is the answer to peace. Once you forgive, there is such a sense of peace, a new beginning, a vibration of such high intensity that the heavens cry with joy. There is nothing more beautiful than a parent who forgives. The stillness that the forgiving parents experience is monumental. It's the liberated bliss, like the release of a balloon into the heavens.

Forgiveness is the end of all uncertainty. There is no more worry and confusion because you experience a true knowing, a connection to the Divine Forever.

In forgiving, you are given the gift of freedom. You free yourself from the illusions of this world that we are somehow separated. It is impossible to be separated from one another because, as I said, We Are All One.

When you forgive, you rid yourself of judgment, and you accept the truth; that only Divine Love is your nature, and this is the God-aspect of yourselves.

The innocence of a child rests in their ability to forgive. Have you ever admired Your Child for forgiving under the most usual circumstances? The younger a child, the more apt they usually are to forgive, for it is our true and highest nature not to blame others or ourselves.

It seems highly predictable that you will want to take responsibility for the passing of Your Child in some form or fashion. I have not met a parent yet who has not tried, in some way, to blame themselves for their child's passing. No matter how illogical the circumstances, parents want to accept the accountability of the passing of their children. Children in Spirit remind me to tell their parents that parents only have had one major duty (relative to their life) and that is the creation of the physical shell in which their soul will be provided its opportunity to develop and grow. Birth is a beautiful gift that you offered to Your Child.

Appreciate the fact that Your Child in Spirit understands that to love is great, but when they leave their physical shell they are not gone. You feel pain but the essence of their true self is with you always.

Happiness is living and expressing Divine Love. "Happiness is not given to you like a birthday present; happiness is created from within," Your Children in Spirit expresses to me. To be happy you must start with creating happy thoughts which will manifest into happy experiences. What you think, you become! Remember a happy thought that you created with Your Child in Spirit. Where did this happy thought come from and what did you manifest with it? Can you recreate it again, right now? Yes! Just try!

It is through these happy thoughts that you will experience Divine Love and, when we become more like a child, we experience the happiness within us.

Joseph conveyed, from Spirit, that when given his building blocks (as a birthday present) it was not the blocks themselves that gave him joy, and it was not even the happiness on Dad's proud face for giving him the blocks; the joy was constructed from within Joseph as his imagination opened to unlimited possibilities of actual structures he could build.

Your Child can provide you with happiness at the expression of their first word, pleasure with their first steps, cheer with their drawings, delight with their singing, but they cannot provide you happiness. You create the joy! You have the power to express happiness at every moment of your conscious life. Happiness is your sacred right and your natural state. You are free to express happiness at any moment. In providing happiness, for yourself, you can offer joy to everyone in your life. There is no difference between love and happiness. Remind yourself of that – everyday!

You are the light of the world and nothing can put this light out. Your dark thoughts and the world's illusions may cause a momentary eclipse but they cannot put out the light within you! Shine bright! The light within you is sufficient to guide you, to enlighten you, to allow you to accept and express Divine Love.

Why wait for heaven, when it is within you already? To be enlightened is to know that God and heaven are within you.

Physical death is actually Spiritual Birth. Many times Children from Spirit want their parents to celebrate their spiritual birthday as a sacred and special day, a day when they get their wings. Through births and deaths, Your Child's soul receives the opportunity to live, express, heal and learn the spiritual lessons which will further their development and growth as a soul. And, as they develop as a soul, they increase their vibration toward heaven and their eventual reunion with God. After their physical life with you, they review their life, and set out plans for their next incarnation. Joy Mills says, "There are only two faces to existence- birth and death-and life survives them both. Just so, sunrise and sunset are not essentially different: it all depends on whether one is facing east or west."

Dorothy from the Wizard of Oz said, *"...if I ever go looking for my heart's desire again, I won't look any further than my own backyard. Because if it isn't there, I never really lost it to begin with! Is that right? There's no place like home. There's no place like home."* Home is where the heart is. Your heart is with Your Child in Spirit. You are home together. Rejoice! And be glad! And again I say, "Rejoice"!

Inspirations and Meditations

Birth is not the beginning. Death is not the end. *Chuang-tsu*

Let life be beautiful like summer flowers and death like autumn leaves. *Tagore*

If you would indeed behold the spirit of death, open your heart wide unto the body of life. For life and death are one, even as the river and the sea are one. *Kahlil Gibran*

Men who have seen life and death …as an unbroken continuum, the swinging of an eternal pendulum, have been able to move as freely into death as they walked through life. *Voltaire*

The thought of death leaves me in perfect peace, for I have a firm conviction that our spirit is a being of indestructible nature; it works on from eternity to eternity…. *Goethe*

The reality of my life cannot die, for I am indestructible consciousness. *Paramahansa Yogananda*

The breaking of forms which we call death releases the consciousness within for the new adventure of building other forms for further growth. *Joy Mills*

Grown-ups never understand anything by themselves, and it is exhausting for children to have to provide explanations over and over again. From *The Little Prince.*

...to bring hope, to bring cheer, to bring joy, yea to bring a smile again to those whose face and heart are bathed in tears and in woe, is making that divine love shine-shine-in thy own soul. Then smile, be joyous, be glad! For the day of the Lord is at hand. *Edgar Cayce*

Love conquers all things... *Virgil*

To love for the sake of being loved is human, but to love for the sake of loving is angelic. *Alphonse de Lamartine*

To love is to receive a glimpse of heaven. *Kren Sunde*

Love goes far beyond what you call the grave. *Edgar Cayce*

Love is but the discovery of ourselves in others, and the delight in the recognition. *Alexander Smith*

Letting the last breath come,
Letting the last breath go.

Dissolving, dissolving into vast space, the light body released from its heavier form. A sense of connectedness with all that is, all sense of separation dissolved in the vastness of being. *Stephen Levine*

Let us not cling to mourning,
Do not stand on my grave and weep.
I am not there
I am not asleep,
I am a thousand winds that blow.
I am the soft stars that shine at night.
"Do not stand on my grave and cry.
I am not there.
I did not die."
J.K. Mohana Rao

Thou causest the wind to blow and the rain to fall. Thou sustainest the living with loving kindness, and in great mercy callest the departed to everlasting life. *Jewish Prayer*

What he had yearned to embrace was not the flesh but a downy spirit, a spark, the impalpable angel that inhabits the flesh. *Wind, Sand and Stars*

Love is not thinking, but being. *Flight to Arras*

The virtue of the candle lies not in the wax that leaves its trace, but in its light. *The Wisdom of the Sands*

Or ever the silver cord be loosed, or the golden bowl be broken, or the pitcher be broken at the fountain, or the wheel broken at the cistern. Then shall the dust return to the earth as it was; and the spirit shall return to God who gave it. *Ecclesiastes 12:1-7*

We find rest in those we love, and we provide a resting place in ourselves for those who love us. *Saint Bernard of Clairvaux*

Your Child's Messages

Please journal the messages you received from Your Child in Spirit as you read this book.

Clairvoyance (signs, symbols and images)

_____

_____

_____

_____

_____

_____

Clairaudience (sounds, words, songs, laughter heard)

_____

_____

_____

_____

_____

Clairsentience (feelings or sensations felt)

_____

_____

_____

_____

_____

_____

Bibliography

Branden, Gregg. *The Spontaneous Healing of Belief Shattering the Paradigm of False Limits.* Carlsbad: Hay House, 2008.

Cayce, Edgar Foundation. *A Search for God Book I.* Virginia Beach: Association for Research and Enlightenment, 1942.

Cayce, Edgar Foundation. *A Search for God Book II.* Virginia Beach: Association for Research and Enlightenment, 1950.

Coelho, Paulo. *The Alchemist.* San Francisco: Harper Collins, 1993.

de Daint-Exupery, Antoine. *The Little Prince.* Orlando: Harcourt, 2000.

McTaggart, Lynne. *The Field: The Quest for the Secret Force of the Universe.* New York: Harper Collins, 2008.

Myss, Caroline. *Anatomy of the Spirit The Seven Stages of Power and Healing.* New York: Three Rivers Press, 1996.

Schwartz, Gary and Russek, Linda. *The Living Energy Universe*. Charlottesville: Hampton Roads Publishing Company, 1999.

Tolle, Eckhart. *Stillness Speaks*. Vancouver: Namaste, 2003.

Van Praagh, James. *Talking to Heaven A Medium's Message of Life After Death*. New York: Penguin Group, 1997.

Vaughan, Frances and Walsh, Roger. *Gifts from A Course in Miracles*. New York:Penguin Putnam, 1995.

Wauters, Ambika. *Chakras and Their Archetypes Uniting Energy Awareness and Spiritual Growth*. Freedom: The Crossing Press, 1998.

Wilde, Stuart. *Miracles*. Carlsbad:Hay House, 1988.

3729922

Made in the USA